ASSIGNMENT: RESCUE

AN AUTOBIOGRAPHY
BY VARIAN FRY

with an introduction
by Dr. Albert O. Hirschman

SCHOLASTIC INC.
New York Toronto London Auckland Sydney

No part of this publication may be reproduced in whole or in part, or stored in a retrieval system, or transmitted in any form or by any means, electronic, mechanical, photocopying, recording, or otherwise, without written permission of the publisher. For information regarding permission, write to Scholastic Inc., 730 Broadway, New York, NY 10003.

ISBN 0-590-46970-3

12 11 10 9 8 7 6 5 4 3 2 1   4   3 4 5 6 7 8/9

Printed in the U.S.A.   01

Contents

Introduction

As I return in my mind to Varian Fry and to the Marseilles days from July to December 1940 when I worked for him, I am struck by how sharply he and those faraway events stand out in my memory. One reason is, of course, the story itself, so vividly told here. Written down in its essentials as soon as Fry returned from France to the United States in 1941, it retains the flavor of immediate reporting. To the readers of this book it will be obvious that there was nothing routine about being associated with Fry and his Centre Américain de Secours. The work was extraordinarily absorbing and often dangerous — and being in danger is always exciting as well as highly memorable.

Moreover, when the story is viewed in its historical context, it looks wholly *improbable*. It starts in June 1940, when the German Army overran France and thus came to rule most of the European continent, from Poland to the Pyrénées. The newly installed French government under Marshal Pétain had signed an abject armistice with Hitler. Article 19 of that document committed the French government to deliver to the Germans any non-French citizen living on French soil who the Germans happened to request. Even before the Holocaust, the Nazis, once in power, were intent on systematically capturing and murdering their most prominent and hated opponents, Jews and non-Jews. Now they had trapped large numbers of these opponents, who had earlier escaped from Germany, in France. Was it conceivable that a lone American citizen, newly arrived from the United States, with just a list of names in his pocket, would be able to keep Article 19 from being carried out with the utmost vigor and dispatch? The playing field was so uneven as to make the prospect of success seem laughable. Yet, we now know that Fry and his Committee actually saved the lives of some two to three thousand people. So, on looking back, the Fry story almost brings to mind the successful fight of David against Goliath, or the Greek myth that pits crafty Ulysses against the huge Cyclops.

It must not be forgotten, of course, that we experienced serious and tragic failures (all described here): the suicide of Walter Benjamin, the extradition of Breitscheid and Hilferding to the Nazis, the miscarriage of early schemes to evacuate our "clients" by boat to North Africa. I remember Varian's reaction to such setbacks. He went through moments of deep despair, which belied the "cool" exterior he so cultivated.

In general, Fry's personality is another unforgettable part of the story. While it comes through here and there in the book, he was like many authors who believe in concealing their emotions. His was a complex character, thoroughly engaging yet full of contradictions. It was endlessly fascinating to try to figure him out. I still remember how, upon leaving the Committee's offices in the evening, with Miriam Davenport or with Hans Sahl, Fry would invariably be our immediate topic of conversation. There was in him a delightful mixture of earnest resolve and of wit, of methodical, almost formal demeanor and of playfulness. His sartorial elegance (his hallmark was a striped dark suit with bow tie), together with his poker face, were tremendous assets to him in dealing with the authorities. The whole operation, from the early days in his room at the Hotel Splendide to the setting up of a well-run regular office with its bureaucratic routine, all of this in the teeth of the French police and, increasingly, as time went on, of the Gestapo, was an act of sheer defiance — how did he get away with it for as long as he did?

I should confess here that I and the other "Europeans" on the Committee occasionally criticized him for being a "typical American," an "innocent abroad." But we had it all wrong. That seeming innocence turned out to be precisely his strength. Had he known from the outset the odds he was up against, he might never have achieved what he did. And in a way he *knew* about this hidden strength of his, and enjoyed the part he played; for, in addition to his other qualities, he was an accomplished actor.

For many years after the war, the staggering achievements of Varian Fry were largely unrecognized in his own country. His death in 1967 (he was only fifty-nine) went almost unnoticed, except for close friends and family. Belatedly, he is now honored for what he was: "a hero for our time."

DR. ALBERT O. HIRSCHMAN

Princeton, August 1992

1
The Secret Mission

"GERMAN ARMIES BLITZKRIEG ACROSS MAGINOT LINE." "FRENCH ARMY ROUTED." "HITLER'S TROOPS ENTER PARIS." "FRANCE FALLS."

So read the headlines in June of 1940. The fuse had been lighted, and soon the powder keg of Europe would explode into total war. In the United States, the rumblings were only beginning to be heard. Most of us still wanted to think of Hitler as the little man with the funny mustache. But there were those of us who knew differently. Some of us had been in Europe during Hitler's rise to power. We had seen, at first hand, that what Hitler *said* was quite different from what he *did*. Behind his good promises he was already scheming to bring the free world to its knees.

In 1935, I had visited Germany and had smelled the air of hatred and oppression Hitler had brought to his country. While in Berlin, I had seen the first great pogrom against the Jews. I saw young Nazi toughs smash up Jewish-owned shops and I watched in horror as they dragged people out into the streets and beat and kicked them. I watched as they drove men and women, cut and bleeding, down the streets, hitting them with clubs, calling them vile names. They knocked down an elderly man and, as he lay on the pavement, the young toughs kicked him in the face again and again.

During this same visit, I talked to a high German official who told me what was in store for all the Jews in Europe. One group in the Nazi party wanted to send them to Palestine or Madagascar. Another group was in favor of exterminating them — murdering every Jew in Europe. Hitler sided with this second group, and since no one argued with Hitler, there was no question that, if he won the war, all the Jews in Europe would be put to death.

Now France had fallen. Paris, which for years had been an escape hatch for men and women fleeing for their lives from revolutions, civil wars, military coups, invading armies, and dictators, was no longer safe. Refugees by the thousands hurried to the unoccupied zone in southern France.

Only after it was too late did they realize they were caught in a trap. A new French government was set up at Vichy under Marshal Philippe Pétain. This puppet governmant signed an armistice with Germany. And in this armistice was the hateful Article 19. This article stated that the French government must "surrender on demand" all refugees from the Greater German Reich. This included not only Germans but Austrians, Czechs, Poles — in fact, anyone the Gestapo wanted to get its hands on was menaced by Article 19.

Then the new Vichy government closed all the French borders and strictly censored all news going out of France. The refugees were now trapped and at the mercy of their enemies. Once they were turned over to the Gestapo, they faced prison, torture, almost certain death in concentration camps.

A group of men and women in New York, shocked by the news of this armistice, got together and formed the Emergency Rescue Committee. Its purpose: to get the artists, writers, musicians, scientists, professors, political figures — men and women whose works and words had made them enemies of the Third Reich — out of France before they were seized by the Gestapo.

Several weeks were spent searching for an agent to send to France. But finding the right person was difficult. France was not giving any entry visas except to diplomats and, now and then, a carefully screened journalist or a social worker sent to help the French refugees. Few people could qualify for a visa under this rule and, of these few, none was willing to risk the dangers of the secret mission.

Since I had a month's vacation coming up in August, I told the Committee, "I'm not right for the job. All I know about being a secret agent, or trying to outsmart the Gestapo, is what I've seen in the movies. But if you can't find anyone else, I'll go."

I was sure the Committee would turn me down.

I didn't know much French, and what little I spoke was with an accent that would quickly mark me as an American. Also, I had no underground or secret agent experience at all.

There was only one thing in my favor. I could get a letter from the International Y.M.C.A. saying they were sending me to France to help the refugees. This letter would get me a visa, and also, once in France, it would serve as a good cover for the operation of smuggling men and women out of the country.

The Committee didn't bite at first. In fact, they tried harder to find someone else. But each day's delay increased the danger to those who were trapped in France. So, after a week or ten days of fruitless search, the Committee called me in. "You're it," I was told. "Get ready to leave at once."

A few days later, I flew from New York to Lisbon. My pockets were full of names of men and women I was to rescue, and my head was full of suggestions from everyone on how to go about it.

But would any of these suggestions work once I was in France, under the very nose of the Gestapo? Friends warned me of the danger. They said I was a fool to go. I, too, could be walking into the trap. I might never come back alive.

But I believed in freedom. I remembered what I had seen in Germany and I knew what would happen to the refugees if the Gestapo got hold of them. Also, I knew that among those trapped in France were many writers, artists, and musicians whose work had given me much pleasure. I didn't know them personally, but I felt a deep love for these people and a gratitude for the many hours of happiness their books and pictures and music had given me. Now they were in danger. It was my duty to help them, just as they — without knowing it — had often helped me in the past.

So it was with a feeling of hope, mixed with a little fear, that I set off on that August day of 1940. In one month, I would have the job done and be back in New York.

Or so I believed.

2
Arrival in Marseilles

Marseilles — the great seaport city in southern France. The streets were crowded with thousands of refugees of every description, fleeing from the north, and the noise and movement were overwhelming. Along with the refugees had come hundreds of demobilized French soldiers dressed in different colored uniforms — brown, blue, and olive drab. The Zouaves wore baggy Turkish-style trousers, and the Senegalese wore gaily colored turbans.

The smells of the city were French — garlic, fish, wine, along with the smell of freshly baked bread, coming from the long, unwrapped loaves people carried home from the bakeries in string bags or in their bare hands.

I got off the crowded train and joined the line of weary passengers inching slowly toward the police inspectors who were checking to make sure everyone had a passport or safe-conduct pass. Anyone who did not would be arrested on the spot.

A policeman took my passport and looked at it. "Aha, an American," he said in a gravel-rough voice.

"Yes," I said, trying to keep my voice calm.

"Marseilles is like your New York City at rush hour, eh?" he said, smiling.

I smiled back. "Quite a mob," I said.

"Refugees. Pouring down from the north," he said. "We would like to pour them back. But the Boches have occupied Paris. So the refugees all run to Marseilles to hide, or maybe sneak across the border. But they won't escape. Sooner or later we arrest all the illegal ones." He smiled again.

"Too bad for them," I said.

"Too bad for them; too bad for us!" He gave me my passport. "Enjoy your stay in our country," he said. "But why you visit us at this unsettled time, I don't know."

His eyes narrowed, and I thought he looked at me suspiciously. But as I went out through the gate, I decided it was my imagination. He knew nothing of the lists in my pockets, nor did he know I had come to smuggle out of France the people whose names were on those lists.

There were no taxis outside the station, but there were plenty of porters. One of them grabbed my suitcases.

"What hotel?" he asked.

"The Splendide," I said.

"Have you a reservation?"

"No," I said.

7

"Then you won't get a room there. The refugees have taken everything in Marseilles. But I know where you can find a place. The Hotel Suisse."

"I'd like to try the Splendide first."

"Très bien," he growled and started to cross the street. I followed him down the great long staircase that led to the Boulevard d'Athènes. At the street level, we turned toward the Hotel Splendide.

The porter was right. There were no rooms available. I left my name and asked them to save me the first room that became available. Then I followed the porter to the Hotel Suisse. I knew he was getting a rake-off from the management there. But then, I had to stay somewhere.

The Suisse was one of those "family" hotels so common in France. It smelled strongly of plumbing drains and garlic. But there was a vacant room, and I took it. The room was in the front of the hotel and faced the railway station, with the wide stairway leading up to it. Beside the stairway was a little park. The room was not too bad.

I made sure the door was locked. Then I unpacked and settled in. After washing off the dust and grime from the train trip, I took my lists and laid them down on the small night table. Over two hundred names of people I was to save. But how was I to do it? How was I to get in touch with them? What could I do for them once I had found them? Now that I was in Marseilles, I suddenly realized that I had no idea how to begin — or where.

I had to find out before it was too late.

3
Conspiracy at the Hotel Splendide

The first person to see was Frank Bohn, whose name had been given to me secretly just before I left New York. The American Federation of Labor had sent Bohn to Marseilles several weeks before to get the European labor leaders, wanted by the Gestapo, out of France.

Bohn had a small room on the third floor of the Hotel Splendide. He opened the door to my knock. When I told him who I was, and why I'd come to France, he grabbed my hand and fairly yanked me into the room.

"I'm so glad you've come, old man," he said, shaking my hand vigorously. "We need all the help we can get. Come in, come in."

There were several German refugees in his room, and they all stood up as I entered. I was somewhat alarmed, and whispered to Bohn, "Is it all right to talk with you here?"

"Yes, indeed, my boy. Everyone here is a friend.

It's safe to say anything you please."

"Well, then," I said, "I'll come right to the point. How do I get my people out? I hope you can tell me."

"Be glad to," Bohn said. He indicated a chair, then sat across from me. "For most of them it's simple," he said. "You see, the disorder and the confusion in Marseilles are working in our favor. The police have too much to do to pay much attention to us. And the Gestapo have not yet arrived in force, which certainly has been a lucky break for us. It's given us time to get many of our refugees across the border."

"But how do you work it?" I asked.

"Well, those who already have an overseas visa can easily get transit visas to travel across Spain and Portugal," he said. "If they have a safe-conduct to show the French police, they can go all the way to the border by train. Those who don't have a safe-conduct take the train to a town not quite so near the frontier as the last stop in France. Either way, they wait until the right moment. Then, when there are no guards around, they cross the border on foot."

"Don't they ever get arrested?" I asked.

"So far nobody has," he said.

One of the refugees spoke up. "Some of the border officials feel sorry for us," he said. "They let us leave France on the train if there is no border guard around to see them do it. But it's a matter of luck. If you happen to run into the right border official, you can go through on the train. If you run into the wrong one, he sends you back. Then you must wait at the frontier until it's safe to go across the border on foot."

"If it's as simple as that," I asked, "why hasn't everyone left France by now?"

"There are several reasons," Bohn said. "Many are still waiting for their overseas visas. Many are still in concentration camps. Some of the leaders don't dare go through Spain. They're afraid they'll be arrested there and deported to Germany."

"Why can't they use false passports?" I asked. "Can't you get them?"

"Oh, we can get false passports, all right," Bohn said. "But the men who are in the greatest danger here don't dare use them. They're afraid they're so well known they'll be recognized before they get five miles into Spain."

"Then how are you going to get these men out?" I asked.

Bohn leaned forward, his face close to mine. "By boat," he said in a loud whisper.

"By boat?"

"It's too early to say more," he said. "But I'm working out a plan. When I have everything sewn up, I'll tell you all about it."

"But what are you using for a cover operation in the meantime?" I asked. "I mean, you need some cover, some explanation to give the police if they get nosey and start asking a lot of questions, don't you?"

Bohn smiled. "In Germany you need a cover, all right. A decoy to keep the police off the scent, to keep them from knowing what you're really up to. But here you don't need one, at least not yet. I've been doing all my business right from this room. So far, I've had no trouble from the police at all."

"You mean you operate openly?" I asked in disbelief.

"Not quite openly," Bohn said. "Some things you must be very secret about — matters such as escapes over the mountains, false passports, and boats. But as far as the refugees on your lists are concerned, it's safe to see them in your room. If anyone asks you what you're doing, you just say you're helping these refugees get their visas and giving them money to live on. This is quite legal, and the French police will not object."

Bohn lowered his voice. "Of course we keep it a dark secret that what we're really doing is getting these people out of the country."

"Then things aren't as bad as people back in the States seem to think," I said.

"Not quite," Bohn said. "But we have to hurry. You never know when things will change. And when they do, you can be sure it will only be for the worse."

4
The Refugees Come —
and the Police

After my talk with Bohn, I felt much better. Now I had a clearer idea of how to go about my rescue work.

Bohn got me a room at the Splendide, and I moved in that very day. Then I sat down and wrote letters to the refugees whose addresses I had. Of course, many of the names on my lists had no addresses, because nobody knew where these people were or what had become of them. But I wrote to the ones I could, asking them to come to the hotel to see me.

They began coming the next day. Many of them had been through hell. Their nerves were shattered and their courage gone. Some of them had been in concentration camps, escaping only at the last moment as the German troops marched through France. They had joined the great crowds of people streaming south. Sometimes they had walked hundreds of miles to get away from the Nazis.

Fortunately, the first refugees to answer my letters were friends of Paul Hagen, a German underground leader I'd met in New York. They were all young, strong, and had plenty of courage. Most of them already had visas to go to America. All they needed was money to make the trip. If they had enough cash to get to Lisbon, they wouldn't be afraid to take their chances with the French and Spanish border police — or the Gestapo in Spain.

I gave them the money they needed and wished them good luck on their way. They thanked me, said good-bye, and immediately took off for the frontier, which they crossed on foot. All of them got to Lisbon safely.

Before leaving, one of these young Germans gave me a map that showed exactly how to cross the frontier. The map showed the cemetery at Banyuls and the path along the cemetery wall that led to the border. A series of crosses marked the boundary line dividing France and Spain, and the route that avoided the French border guards was shown by arrows. I hid this map of the escape route behind the mirror on my closet door, knowing it would come in handy.

By the end of my first week in Marseilles, word had spread all over the unoccupied zone that an American had arrived from New York, like an angel from heaven. His pockets were stuffed with money and he could get passports, visas, or documents of any sort, for anyone who needed them. I was even told there was a man in a town far to the west of Marseilles who was selling my name and address to the refugees, for fifty francs per refugee!

Of course it wasn't true that my pockets were stuffed with money, or that I could get the necessary passports, visas, or other documents. But the refugees believed it anyway and they began coming to the hotel in droves — not just the people on my lists, but anyone who thought I could help.

By the end of my second week in Marseilles, there were so many people waiting outside my door that the hotel management complained, saying everyone must wait downstairs in the lobby and come up to my room one at a time. But soon the lobby was packed with people waiting to see me. Then, with a great clanging of its bell, the paddy wagon came along, and the police picked them all up. They took them to the station house and questioned them about me and my activities. After the questioning, the refugees were allowed to leave.

When I heard about this, I decided to go at once and see the Chief of Police. I would show him my letter from the International Y.M.C.A. and explain that I was helping the refugees to get their overseas visas and giving them money to live on while they waited. Since this was legal and true, even if it was a cover operation for my other work, I would ask for his permission to continue my service. As for the secret part of my work — well, I would not tell him about that.

And may he never find out about it until long after I've left France, I said to myself. I crossed my fingers and was about to knock on wood when the telephone rang.

It was Frank Bohn.

"It's the police, old man," he said in a loud stage whisper. "We had to expect this. I'm going down now. You'd better check your room for any signs of our illegal work. Destroy any evidence. I'll stall them off until you get here. But hurry!"

It was too late. But, as I hung up the phone, I knocked on wood anyway.

5

Destroying
the Evidence

I locked the door to my room and emptied the contents of my pockets onto the bed. I gathered together all the little slips of paper that gave the addresses of places where refugees in danger could hide, maps of escape routes, notes of names of underground workers and how to contact them.

Also, I had a record of all the dollars I'd exchanged for francs on the black market. I threw this on the pile. Then I grabbed my briefcase and went through it, then the desk, then the dresser drawers.

I found papers with the names of people who could be contacted on each side of the border, deep in Spain, and even in Portugal. I had listed all the people who had so far escaped, with the addresses of where they were living in Lisbon while waiting for a ship to the United States. I checked in books and behind books, in the empty suitcases, and in the boxes under the bed for any false visas or identity cards, or forged passports. Luckily, there were none.

When I had everything piled on the bed, I picked it up and went into the bathroom. Quickly, I tore all the papers into small pieces and flushed them down the toilet.

When I had finished, only two innocent documents were left. One was my own American passport — genuine; the other was my letter from the International Y.M.C.A. — also genuine. That was all.

Except, of course, for the lists of names I'd brought from the States. And these were far from innocent. They gave the names of all the refugees I was to get out of France. They also gave the code names I used in cables and letters to the Emergency Rescue Committee in New York: "Eloise" for Germany, "Heinrich" for France, "Ursula" for Great Britain, and so forth.

If I destroyed my lists, I'd be out of business, even without help from the police. But I couldn't let these lists fall into their hands. Not only would they have proof of my illegal activities, but they'd arrest everyone else whose name was on the lists.

What could I do? Where could I hide them? Then I remembered where I'd hidden the map of the escape route across the frontier from France to Spain. I had no time to lose: The telephone might ring at any moment. So I quickly got out my pocket knife, and with the back of the blade started to take out the screws that held the mirror to the closet door. When I had enough of them out to pull the wood panel away from the door, I smoothed out the lists and slipped them behind the mirror. Then I put the screws back, one by one. I had to be very careful now. If the knife slipped, it would leave a telltale scratch on the wood. I felt the sweat pouring off my forehead. It seemed to take hours to turn each screw carefully into place.

I had almost finished the last one when the phone rang. Slowly, trying not to hurry, not to slip, I got the last screw tight. Then I made a dash for the ringing telephone.

"*On vous demande en bas*," the dry voice of the hotel clerk said. "The police want you to come downstairs for questioning immediately."

"I'll be right down," I said.

I wiped the sweat off the palms of my hands and off my forehead. Then I closed the closet door, looked at the mirror, and quickly checked around the room. I pulled down my jacket sleeves, took one good deep breath, and went downstairs.

6
Squaring It
with the Police

As I got off the elevator, the room clerk nodded toward the writing room. I walked as bravely as I could toward the door.

The "police" turned out to be one inspector. He must have finished questioning Frank Bohn, for he was alone in the writing room. Dressed in a dark business suit, he looked more like a salesman who had come to sell me a life insurance policy than a detective who was there to arrest me. He was very polite and said he was sorry for calling on me at such an early hour. Then he asked me to sit down. After we were both seated, he started to ask questions about my credentials, why I was in Marseilles, and what work I was doing here.

First I showed him my passport. Then I showed him my letter from the International Y.M.C.A. He read this through slowly several times and made some notes about it in his notebook. Then he folded the letter and gave it back to me. I explained that

I had been sent to Marseilles to make a study of the needs of the refugees. Also, I said, I was giving small sums of money to those who needed it to live on. The inspector didn't say a word about false passports or smuggling refugees into Spain — nor did I.

After about fifteen minutes, he said, "Well, I can see nothing wrong. You have a proper letter from a neutral organization. Everything you are doing seems to be legal."

"Oh, I assure you it is," I said.

"We get many reports at Police Headquarters," he said. "People who are angry because their requests for visas are turned down, people who want to collect a reward for turning in a secret agent or spy, people who will squeal on anyone just to get in good with the police. You understand, we have to check out all these reports, in case some high official of the government in Vichy starts asking questions."

He paused. His voice became very low. "If I had found anything suspicious, it would be necessary for me to arrest you here and now."

He paused again, looking me straight in the eye. "You understand?" he said.

I stared back at him. Then I nodded. "Yes, I understand."

I understood, all right. This man was on my side. He was telling me that as a police inspector he had found nothing wrong with my answers. But, as a Frenchman, he knew I was up to a lot more than I'd told him about. His quiet "You understand?" was a warning. A warning to be much more careful than I had been up to now. Otherwise, I'd land in prison and be expelled from the country, or worse.

He turned to pick up his hat. "Sad days have fallen on France," he said. "It is very bad for the refugees. Especially those wanted by the Gestapo. Soon we will have to pick many of them up. Arrest them. Surrender them to the Nazis."

He turned back to me. "I am glad you are helping them," he said. Then he added quickly, "By giving them money, I mean."

He apologized once again for the early hour of his visit. Then he shook my hand and left.

I waited until he went out the main door of the hotel. Then I hurried up to Frank Bohn's room.

Bohn's talk with the police inspector had been much like mine. Bohn felt as I did, that the inspector was trying to warn us. We had made a serious mistake by not going to the police at the very beginning.

Maybe it wasn't too late to square ourselves. But there was no time to lose. We must go to the police at once and explain the relief part of our mission in Marseilles. If we got their approval for that, at least our cover operation would be legal and we would no longer be under suspicion. The police would stop watching us so closely. I called Police Headquarters and made an appointment for the next day.

When we arrived at the Police Headquarters, we were shown into the office of a high official, the Secretary General. After we were seated, he resumed his chair behind the formal desk. His manner was correct, but very frosty.

"Now gentlemen," he said, "what did you want to see me about?"

We explained that we had been sent to France to aid the refugees. We said we would very much appreciate police permission to set up a small committee to help us in this work.

"The French authorities would welcome such a committee," he said coldly, "*if* it does nothing illegal." He eyed us warily and added, "And I must strongly stress the word *if*."

We both acted surprised and hurt at the very idea that we would even think of doing anything illegal. He seemed convinced and gave us permission to set up our committee.

Now my underground work had a cover operation — The American Relief Center was the name we gave our committee. And the Center had the official approval of the police authorities.

I still worked from my room at the Hotel Splendide. Legally, I saw hundreds of refugees, in addition to those named on my lists. Illegally, I worked at getting the people I had been sent to rescue out of France. In many cases, this meant getting them false passports or forged visas. While we waited for their papers, I showed these people my lists and asked if they knew the whereabouts of any of the other people whose names were on them. In this way, I got many of the addresses I was looking for. I learned that some of my people had already gotten out of France, so I crossed their names off my lists.

There were other names I had to cross off, too, but for a very different reason.

Luis Companys, former leader of the non-Communist trade unions in Catalonia, Spain, had been arrested by the Gestapo and taken to Spain. There he was turned over to Franco's henchmen, who choked him to death by winding a fine piano wire around his neck and pulling both ends tight.

Ernst Weiss, a Czech novelist, had taken poison when the Germans entered Paris.

Walter Hasenclever, a German playwright, had killed himself with an overdose of sleeping pills in a French detention camp.

Karl Einstein, an art critic, had been caught trying to cross the Spanish frontier and had been turned back. Having neither the strength nor the courage to wait and try again, he hanged himself.

The rotting body of Willi Muenzenberg, a political enemy of Hitler's Third Reich, was found hanging from a tree near Grenoble, where it had been for more than a week.

One by one, I sadly crossed off the names of the men and women on my lists who had met one kind of horrible death or another. But almost every day I got at least one address or promising lead that might help me find those still alive.

When I got all their papers together, forged and legal, and the refugees were ready to go, I gave them enough money to get to Lisbon. Then I took the map of the frontier from its hiding place behind my mirror and showed them exactly how to cross the border into Spain. And they were off.

All the refugees used the same route in those first few weeks and they all got safely to Lisbon. It was as simple as that.

Obviously, this was too good to last.

7

Beamish, Franzi, and Lena

Every morning at eight o'clock the grind started again, and went right on until almost midnight. There was no letup. Each day was busier than the day before, with more people to see and more impossible decisions to make.

I couldn't help every refugee in France; there were too many of them. Deciding whom to help and whom not to help was one of the toughest jobs of all. I had no way of knowing who was really in danger and who wasn't. The only thing to do was to give each refugee the full benefit of the doubt. Otherwise, I might refuse help to someone and learn too late that he had been dragged off to a death camp. But, for the most part, I stuck closely to the names on my list.

Soon there were too many refugees for one person to interview. I had to get help. That's where "Beamish" came in. He was the first person to work for me in Marseilles. Beamish was a refugee from

Hitler's Germany — intelligent, good-natured, and always cheerful. I started calling him "Beamish" because of his impish eyes and constant pout, which he could turn into a big grin in an instant. His only fault was his absentmindedness. When I spoke to him, it was sometimes as much as twenty seconds before he gave any sign of having heard me. As he himself said, he was *un peu dans la lune* — a little in the clouds.

Beamish was only twenty-five, but he was a veteran of two wars, and he'd had a lot of experience with underground work. He'd fought with the Republican Army in the Spanish Civil War for nearly a year and then, when World War II broke out, he had enlisted in the French Army. When the French were defeated, Beamish was in a bad spot. If the Nazis got him, they would shoot him as a traitor.

Luckily, Beamish's lieutenant was very understanding. Just before the armistice, he called Beamish in. "I am going to make you a French citizen," he said. "It will save you from the revenge of the Boches."

He then told Beamish to pick a new name, birthplace, and birth date. Beamish picked the name Albert Hermant, and decided to be born in Philadelphia. I asked him why he chose Philadelphia.

"It is one of the few places in America I knew the name of," he said with a grin. "Besides, I figured birth records in the little town of Philadelphia would be hard to check."

His expression changed when I told him that

Philadelphia was a large city, and probably one of the first cities in the United States to keep careful records of births and other vital statistics.

When Beamish had picked his name and birthplace, his lieutenant made out a new set of military papers to replace his old ones. After signing and stamping them, he said to Beamish, "O.K., Albert Hermant, now go get lost in the crowds."

Beamish stuck the old papers listing his real name in a tin can and buried it in a field. Then he headed south on his bicycle, passing columns of German soldiers on the way.

When he arrived in the unoccupied zone, he got army discharge papers in his new name. Instead of a birth certificate, he received something called a "certificate of life," which was given to him by the Mayor of the city. It read, "We, the Mayor, certify that Mr. Albert Hermant, born in Philadelphia, Pennsylvania, is alive because he stood before us today."

You could have searched Beamish from head to foot and found no trace of his real name anywhere. But he had papers and cards of every kind with his new name on them. Besides his discharge papers, his identity card, and his "certificate of life," he had membership cards in the Auberges de Jeunesse, a French youth hostel outfit, the Club de Sans Club, a kind of tourist club for people without a club, and half a dozen other cards from various French organizations.

Beamish would smile and say in his German-accented English, "I've overdone it, I guess. I have so many papers, the police would suspect me right away. I'm like a criminal with too many alibis. I should get rid of some of them."

But he never did. He loved them too much, just because they were all so grandly false.

My second helper, however, spoke English like an upperclass Englishman. He was an Austrian, named Franz von Hildebrand, but we all called him Franzi. He had gone to Williams College in Williamstown, Massachusetts, and though he spoke English elegantly, his sentences were laced with American slang, quite a bit of it profane.

"Well for Godsake," he'd say when I'd been out on an errand and come back late, "whereinhell have you been? I thought you'd fallen through." Or, "Damnitall, Fry, howinhell do you expect us to work when you don't come back after lunch? We thought you'd been nabbed by the cops."

Franzi was a Catholic who believed the best form of government was a monarchy. The Austrian Social Democrats, who did not believe in a monarchy and who thought I should have only Social Democrats helping me, were upset to see Franzi working in my room. But I was equally concerned about Catholics, Monarchists, and Social Democrats in danger in France, so I refused to take sides in the endless arguments between the Right and the Left. Also, I didn't want the police to think I was helping only Socialists, since the French had outlawed the Socialist Party. Franzi was good insurance against this risk.

Centuries before Franzi was born, Switzerland

had given the von Hildebrand family honorary Swiss citizenship. So Franzi had a Swiss passport, making him a citizen of a neutral country, even though he was Austrian by birth. After Vichy signed the armistice with the Nazis, it seemed wise for him to pass only as a Swiss citizen and forget about being an Austrian. With his blue eyes, blond hair, and neatly trimmed mustache, he easily got away with it. This was a big help to us.

Franzi was also very helpful to us in many other ways. For one thing, he had worked with an Austrian refugee committee in Paris before the occupation, so he knew, as Beamish and I did not, how a relief committee should be run. He also knew many of the refugees who came to me for help, but who were not on my lists. He could advise me whether those refugees were trustworthy, or if they were police stooges and Gestapo spies.

The third helper to join us was Lena Fishman. Before the occupation, Lena had been a professional social worker in Paris. She could speak half a dozen languages, and in addition to being able to speak and write Russian, Polish, and Spanish, she could take shorthand equally fast in English, French, and German. When we finally managed to buy a typewriter — at an outrageous price — Lena spent all day typing answers to the hundreds of letters we received. If she had a free moment, she would also help us interview the refugees.

Lena was very lively and good-natured and had an almost magical power of calming the refugees when they became excited. I could never figure out just what her magic was, but part of it was the phrase, *"Il ne faut pas exagérer."* In English it means, "You must not go too far." I don't know why, but these words always calmed an excited refugee, even when he or she was hysterical.

Lena was always mixing up her languages when she talked. At the end of the day, for instance, when she was ready to go home, and was freshening her makeup, she would say, *"Je me fais une petit beauté* (I'll just freshen up.) and I'll leave you." Just like that, half in French, half in English.

With my three helpers — Beamish the outside man, Franzi the interviewer, and Lena the secretary — we interviewed those who came to seek our help all day long. We wrote their names down on white file cards, but we never listed their addresses. In case of a sudden raid by the police, we did not want a lot of cards lying around with addresses where people could be picked up and arrested.

In the evening, when all the refugees had finally gone, Beamish, Franzi, Lena, and I would hold a staff meeting. We would go over all the cards for that day and try to decide what action to take on each case. Since we were always afraid the police might plant a hidden microphone in the room, we discussed all secret subjects in the bathroom, where we turned all the water faucets on full. We figured the noise of the water would make a recording sound like one long thunderstorm and not a word of what we said could be understood.

Secret subjects included false passports, false identity cards, false residence permits, and false safe-conduct passes. They also included secret escape routes over the Pyrénées Mountains into Spain and the names of those refugees who were in the greatest immediate danger from the Gestapo.

We couldn't cable these names to New York. We couldn't even mention them in a letter, because all letters were opened and read by a censor. So Lena typed out our secret messages on narrow sheets of thin paper. Then Beamish, Franzi, and I pasted the ends of the papers together and, when the paste was dry, we made the long strips into tight rolls. We put each roll into a rubber finger and tied the end with a thin thread. Then we opened the bottom of a partly used tube of toothpaste or shaving cream. We pushed the rubber-covered packages well up into the tube. After we closed the end of the tube, we rolled it up a little way, so it would look as if it were in daily use. Whenever a refugee we trusted was leaving France, we sent the tube with him and asked him to mail the roll to New York when he reached Lisbon. All our secret messages got safely through to New York, and the police never caught on to our toothpaste trick.

There was only one trouble with the toothpaste method of sending secret messages. It was very slow. So, to save time, if a refugee agreed that it was safe to do so, we cabled his name to New York, but never his address. Thus, our final job each evening was to type up and send a daily cable. When it was ready, Beamish and I would take it down the dark, narrow street to the police station. There I had to show my passport to a police officer to prove

I was the one who had signed the cable. Then we went to the post office, where we sent the cable off to New York.

One night Beamish and I made our trip later than usual. The street lights, painted dark blue, went so dim they might as well have been turned off altogether. We had finished at the post office and were making our weary way back to the Splendide. Just as we turned the corner, we saw a big black Mercedes pull up in front of the hotel. Beamish and I jumped back into the shadows and flattened ourselves against the wall. The Mercedes stopped, and a chauffeur got out. He ran around and opened the rear door of the car. As he stood at attention, five German officers got out of the car. They were wearing long gray overcoats, peaked caps turned up in front, like the wrong end of a duck, black kid gloves, and shiny black leather boots. Under the peaks of their caps, we could make out the gilt eagles and swastikas of Adolf Hitler's Third Reich.

"Heil Hitler," they said, as they clicked their heels and gave the Nazi salute.

"Heil Hitler," the chauffeur said, as he stood at rigid attention and returned the salute.

The officers turned and went through the revolving door into the Hotel Splendide.

My voice was not very steady as I looked at Beamish and whispered, "Well, it looks like the Gestapo has arrived in full force."

Beamish nodded. "Now the fun begins," he said.

8
We Move
to the Rue Grignan

We waited until we were sure the German officers had gone up to their rooms. Then we went into
the hotel. It was very late, and the bar was closed,
but we persuaded the night porter to get us two
small glasses of brandy to steady our nerves.

As we sipped our brandy, we agreed on one
thing. We would have to move our office. We
couldn't ask refugees, already terrified of the Gestapo, to come to a hotel where they were likely to
run into German officers wearing the swastika-
decorated uniform of the Third Reich. Nor did I,
myself, have the courage or desire to be working
so close to them, either.

Only a few days before, I had met a man who
sold pocketbooks, billfolds, and leather novelties in
a small shop on the Rue Grignan. But he had seen
the writing on the wall and decided to give up his
business before it was too late.

I went to see him first thing next morning and

told him about the arrival of the German officers.

"Clancy has lowered the boom," he said.

I was astonished to hear this expression from him, and I must have looked it, for he laughed and said, "I learned that from some American tourists who came into my shop before the war. It is from a funny song."

"Oh, yes," I said. "It's an old American song."

"Now the Germans have lowered the boom," he said seriously, "but that is not very funny. I, too, know the terror that strikes the heart at the sight of the Nazis in their cold and elegant battle dress, covered with swastikas."

"You are a Jew?" I asked.

"Yes," he said. "I know what is coming to those of my faith. That is why I am selling out all my merchandise while there is still time. But the rent on my quarters is paid through the end of the year. I would be more than happy for you to occupy them, rent free, until then."

I thanked him for his kind offer and told him that it would certainly solve one of my immediate problems.

"Do not thank me," he said. "It is little enough I can do to help out in the good work you are doing for the refugees."

So we moved into the second floor of the old building on the Rue Grignan right away, which for several days was a confusion of refugees, pocketbooks, packing cases, and moving men. But before long, the merchandise, counters, and shelves of the pocketbook business had been replaced with the desks and chairs of the relief business. And we did not have the cold, hard eyes of German officers watching our every move.

With the opening of the new office, the crowds of frantic refugees grew larger than ever, and we had to find someone to handle the traffic in the waiting room and in the hall and stairs outside. That's when we found Charles Fawcett. Charlie, whom everyone in Marseilles called Shar-lee, had served in the American Volunteer Ambulance Corps before the armistice. Now he became our doorman and reception clerk.

Charlie was from Georgia, and before the war he had been studying art in Paris. I often wondered how far Charlie would go in his chosen field, since his idea of art seemed to consist only of drawing pretty girls, preferably nude. He had many girl friends, and there was always at least one of them in the office as long as Shar-lee worked for us.

As a doorman, Charlie had one great drawback. He couldn't speak anything but English, and most of the refugees didn't speak any English at all. But his ambulance-driver's uniform impressed them, and his good nature cheered them all. Even if the refugees didn't understand what he said, they all liked him. In fact, he was the most popular member of our staff.

Beamish's work kept him out of the office most of the time. Lena spent all day keeping track of the correspondence and typing letters. I was busy with appointments both inside and outside the office. That left only one full-time interviewer, Franzi.

And the crowds had now grown so big he could not handle them all. We had to get more interviewers. That is how Miriam Davenport came into our lives.

Miriam, a graduate of Smith College, had gone to Paris to study art. After the fall of Paris, she joined the exodus to Marseilles. On her way south, she met Walter Mehring, a German poet who was wanted by the Gestapo because of his anti-Nazi writings. He did not dare come to the office himself, so he sent Miriam with a message for me. I made an appointment with her to meet Mehring outside the office and, before she left, I asked her to join our staff. She immediately accepted.

Miriam spoke fluent French and German, and her knowledge of art and artists made her most helpful to us. If a refugee came to us claiming to be an artist, and Miriam had not heard of him, she would send him out to make a drawing. When he brought the drawing back, she would look at it and decide right away whether or not he was telling the truth.

Miriam was always either laughing or coughing, and Frank Bohn worried a good deal about her health.

"I tell you," he said, "that girl has TB. I don't like that cough at all. You should send her away for a good rest."

But Miriam was too busy working for us. She only went on laughing when she wasn't coughing.

There was a lot of noise, a lot of confusion, and each day our problems seemed to increase. But at least we now had a fairly smooth-running office, and things were looking up.

There was only one problem. August was over, and we were well into September. My month in France was up. It seemed I had hardly made a dent in my rescue work. But how much longer could I stay? Well, I figured, only time, the police, and the Germans can answer that. Meantime, I must speed up my underground work. I must get as many of my people out of France as quickly as I can, even if it means taking bigger and bigger risks.

9
We Deal
with Gangsters

We had three problems to solve, all at the same time. One was to locate new sources of false passports. The second was to get false identity cards that would pass for real. The third was to find some way to get large sums of money into France from New York, without the police knowing about it.

Beamish solved all three of these problems. He got Polish passports from the Polish Consul in Marseilles, and Lithuanian passports from the Lithuanian Consul in Aix-en-Provence. He even found a way to get beautiful Chinese visas. Everything on these visas was printed in Chinese except the words "100 francs." Of course, none of us could read them, but someone who knew Chinese later told me what they said: "The person carrying this visa shall not be allowed to enter China under any circumstances." Fortunately, the Portuguese Consul couldn't read Chinese any better than we could. He gave anyone who had a Chinese entry visa a transit visa through Portugal, so we got away with it.

As for false identity cards, Beamish turned up a little Viennese artist who called himself Bill Freier. Bill had been a popular cartoonist before the war, but when the war started he had been thrown into a concentration camp because of some of his unflattering cartoons of Hitler and the Nazis. He later escaped and fled to Marseilles, where he was now hiding out. Bill was a likeable fellow who really wanted to help his fellow refugees. At the same time he wanted to make enough money to keep himself and his girl friend, Mina, alive. Bill and Mina were very much in love. They wanted to get married and go to the United States to live.

Bill would buy blank identity cards at a tobacco shop, fill them in, and then paint on the rubber stamp that made them official. He was so skillful with his paintbrush that only an expert could tell the difference. Bill charged us only fifty cents for each identity card, and we made great use of his services. We also added his name, and Mina's, to our list of people to get out of France, and cabled New York to ask the Committee to get them visas.

The story of how Beamish solved our money problem is much more involved. It led to our meeting and dealing with the gangsters of Marseilles.

Beamish was very fond of women. Although his favorite girl friend was in Paris. Paris was far away, so in Marseilles Beamish was going out with a blue-eyed blonde who worked at the American Consulate. Through her he met a businessman, named Malandri, from Corsica. Since almost all Corsicans hate Italians, Beamish was sure Malandri was not an agent for Mussolini. And, since he wasn't, Beamish figured he couldn't be a Gestapo agent, either.

Beamish told Malandri about our money problem. The $3,000 in cash I had brought with me from New York was gone. If the Committee cabled me more money, the police would know about my receiving it. They could call me in at any time and ask where I was spending so much money. I couldn't very well explain, since most of it was going for my illegal work.

"I've got the answer for you," Malandri said, and he took Beamish to see Charles.

In public life, Charles owned a very popular restaurant called the Dorade. Marseilles businessmen, refugees from Paris, and American relief workers ate there every day. In private life, however, Charles was head of Marseilles's leading group of Corsican gangsters. While he sat behind the cash register at the Dorade and ran his restaurant, he was conducting all the illegal affairs of his gang. These affairs consisted of white slavery, black market dealings, and smuggling dope.

When Beamish first talked with Charles, he ran into a stone wall. Charles didn't trust Americans.

"Fry and his Committee are Americans," he said. "I won't do business with them."

It seems that some years before, Charles had gone to the United States. Something, no one knew what, but something had soured him against all Americans. Perhaps he had been double-crossed by some American gangsters who were smarter — or more crooked — than he was. Or perhaps it was just that an American girl had jilted him. In any case, Charles had returned to Marseilles with a definite dislike for Americans.

"They are not honest," he kept saying. "I tell you, these guys would rob their own mothers."

Though Charles did not want to have any dealings with Americans, he always liked the idea of making a profit. In the end, he found a way to make his profit and still not deal with us directly. He introduced Beamish to Dimitru.

Dimitru was a short, oily little man, with over-polite manners, who could turn his smile on and off like an electric light. When you shook his right hand, it felt like an empty glove. But he knew a lot of people who were eager to get money out of France before it was too late. So Beamish, Dimitru, and Charles made a deal.

Dimitru would take Beamish to see a client with money. Beamish would get the name of the client's lawyer or agent in New York. Then we would arrange for our Committee in New York to pay so many dollars to the agent or lawyer named by the client. For these dollars, paid in America, the client gave us francs in France. This way we were supplied with money without having the police know anything about it.

Dimitru always knew people who wanted to change francs to dollars, so for many months our money problem was solved. During all that time, Dimitru never failed to give prompt and honest service. Of course, he was getting a cut on every deal, that he split three ways. One third went to himself, one third went to Charles, and one third went to Beamish. Beamish always took his third. He knew that if he didn't, Dimitru and Charles would either think he was crazy or that he was pulling something crooked. But Beamish always turned his cut over to me to use in helping more refugees.

"Easy come, easy go," Beamish would say with a laugh, as he passed over the francs. "First I was a soldier. Then I was an underground smuggler. Now I am a gangster. What next?"

"Who knows," I said. "Maybe next you'll be a Hollywood movie star. A glamour boy, the idol of millions."

"Ah, with all those beautiful girls chasing me," Beamish said with his big grin. "I'd like that. Yes, that's what I want to be next."

But Beamish didn't get his wish. We were going along smoothly but, without knowing it, we were heading right into a great big storm.

10
Everything
Goes Wrong

The storm broke when Miriam Davenport's friend, Walter Mehring, set out for the frontier.

Mehring was one of the best of the modern German poets, but he did not make a very impressive appearance. In fact, he was so small that we called him "Baby." He had only one soiled, unpressed suit, the same one he was wearing when he arrived in Marseilles. He looked more like a tramp than a poet — or a baby.

He had papers to travel through Spain, but he would not go because he was afraid of being recognized and arrested by the Gestapo. Finally, I got him a false Czech passport, under another name. Baby took the train for the border immediately.

He had to change trains en route. When he got off the first train he was surprised and pleased to see there was no police check at the railway station. So he went to an outdoor café to celebrate his forthcoming escape.

In less than five minutes, he was picked up by a plainclothesman. The detective thought Baby was the petty thief and purse snatcher the town police had been looking for for six months. At the police station, however, they discovered Mehring was a foreigner traveling without a safe-conduct pass. They ordered him sent to the nearby concentration camp of St. Cyprien, the pesthole of France.

Mehring had two sets of papers on him — his legitimate American visa and his false Czech passport. Fortunately, the police did not search him at the police station. So, on the train to the camp, he asked permission to go to the toilet. Once inside, he tore up his false papers and flushed them down the john. His beautiful Czech passport, with all its lovely visas, was scattered in small pieces along the railroad tracks of southern France.

When we got word of Mehring's arrest, we immediately hired a lawyer to handle his case. We never learned exactly how the lawyer managed it, but a few days later the head of the camp called Mehring into his office and gave him an unsigned release order. He said he was sorry but he couldn't sign the order without direct authorization from Vichy.

Baby took the hint. He picked up the release order and got out of there. The order worked just as well without a signature as with one!

When Mehring got back to Marseilles, his residence permit had expired. Since it was vital to have a residence permit, I went at once to see the lawyer. He took me to the Chief of the Bureau of Foreign

Residents, a Monsieur Barellet. Barellet was very pleasant and said that all Baby needed was a doctor's certificate stating that he had been too ill to apply for a new residence permit at the time the old one expired. Barellet even gave me the name of the doctor to see.

It worked beautifully. We put Baby to bed in a room at the Hotel Splendide. The doctor came over, barely glanced at Baby, and then signed a very impressive certificate. It said that Mehring had been too ill to call at Police Headquarters for an extension of his residence permit at the time it expired. It added that Baby would continue to be too ill to leave his room until mid-November.

I took the signed certificate back to Barellet and he gave Mehring a two-month extension right away. This was unheard of for a non-French refugee. Usually they got only two weeks at a time, at the very most.

It happened that I hit Barellet at a good moment. Two Gestapo agents had just paid him a visit and spent the entire morning looking into his files and questioning his subordinates about Barellet's politics and the way he ran his office. This had made Barellet furious. His feelings and his pride were hurt.

"Those so-and-sos," he said. "All morning long they were nosing into my business. Ordering me around like I was a complete idiot. Then, before they left, they gave me a list of three names. 'Arrest these three foreigners as quickly as you can, or things will go tough with you,' they said. How dare they talk to me that way?"

"May I see the list they gave you?" I asked.

Barellet picked up a small piece of paper from his desk and handed it to me. Written in pencil, in a German hand, were the names of Prince Ernst Ridiger von Starhemberg, Georg Bernhard, and Max Braun. All three were anti-Nazis who had opposed Hitler when he first came to power. Now Hitler wanted his revenge.

I made a careful mental note of the three names and then handed the list back to Barellet.

"Happily, we don't know where these men are," he said. "But if you do, get word to them at once to beat it." He paused for a moment, then went on. "There are two others they will soon ask us to arrest, though. Breitscheid and Hilferding. And how can we not do it? Like everyone else in Marseilles, the police know where they are. Every day they sit in the same café on the Boulevard d'Athènes. Don't they know they are endangering all the other refugees by their behavior?" he said angrily. "You can tell them both I said so, if you like."

Rudolf Breitscheid and Rudolf Hilferding were Frank Bohn's problem. Breitscheid had been one of the most important men in Germany before Hitler became dictator. In fact, Breitscheid had been one of the leaders of one of the parties that opposed der Fuehrer. Now he was one of Hitler's most hated enemies.

In the early days, Hilferding had been the German Minister of Finance. But he, too, had opposed Hitler. Now, like Breitscheid, he was high on the list of enemies Hitler wanted eliminated.

Both Breitscheid and Hilferding had American visas, but both felt they were so well known they'd be recognized instantly in Spain. So they didn't dare take the Spanish escape route. Instead, they were waiting for Bohn to complete his boat plan so that they could escape by sea.

After leaving Barellet's office, I went straight back to the Splendide to see Frank Bohn. I told him what Barellet had said. Bohn was as alarmed as I was. We both went across the street to the café where the two men always sat at the same table. There we laid it on the line, telling them exactly what Barellet had said.

"You are both in very great danger," we told them.

But they refused to move.

"It's ridiculous," Breitscheid said. "Hitler wouldn't dare ask for our surrender. The whole German working class would rise in revolution if he did."

And the two old men continued to sit in the same café every day, although now both of them carried vials of poison in their vest pockets, just in case.

Of the three men on Barellet's list, we knew that Prince von Starhemberg was in London. So, we believed, although we did not know for sure, was Max Braun. As for Georg Bernhard, we didn't know any more about his whereabouts than the Gestapo did. So, while Barellet's news about the Gestapo's visit to his office shook us up a bit, it made us feel good to realize that the Gestapo wasn't nearly as well informed as it was reputed to be.

A few days after Mehring's arrest, we got another piece of bad news. A postcard from Spain that had been stamped by the Spanish military censor said that five of our refugees had been arrested there. They were now in prison in Spain, and they were asking us to get them out. The postcard didn't say why they'd been arrested. Were their names on the Gestapo's wanted list? Or had they gone too far into Spain without reporting to the border guard? We didn't know, and we had no way of finding out.

Nevertheless, we decided to cut the chances of any more arrests. Instead of letting the refugees go through Spain alone, we now sent them down to the frontier in groups, with an experienced underground worker in charge. This was a big risk for us. If they were caught, we could no longer claim we had nothing to do with helping refugees get out of France. But sending them in groups with a guide reduced the chances of their being caught. And our first duty was to the refugees, not ourselves.

Whenever an experienced underground worker was ready to leave, we made up a party of refugees to go with him. When there was no experienced underground worker leaving, we sent the refugees down to the frontier with an American named Richard Ball.

Dick Ball had been a friend of Charlie Fawcett's in the Ambulance Corps. He had been in France for years, earning his living as a traveling salesman of lard! He knew the country backwards and forwards, and spoke a very vulgar French — so fluently that not even the most suspicious Frenchman would ever have taken him for an American. Dick was more than glad to help anyone anywhere he could, and for a long time he was one of the most valuable members of our little band of conspirators. He would make trips to the frontier every other day or so, taking two or three refugees with him. Once there, he made sure they got safely across the border into Spain without being arrested. Then he would come back for the next batch.

Early one morning, I was having breakfast in my hotel room when someone knocked loudly on my door. Thinking it was the police, I made a quick dive to hide my papers. But the door opened before I could get my hands on them.

It was Frank Bohn. He was more excited than I'd ever seen him, and he talked so loudly I was afraid someone would call the police. I tried to quiet him down even before I understood what he was talking about.

"They've got it, old man," he said.

"Got what?" I asked.

"The boat," he said. "What else? The boat!"

The boat was Bohn's escape ship. With it he was going to rescue all his protégés who could not go through Spain, in one daring dash to the British stronghold of Gibraltar. It was the plan he'd been so excited and secretive about the first day I talked to him at the Splendide. For weeks he'd been planning, scheming, arranging this one grand plan. Now it had backfired.

Bohn was pacing around the room like a caged tiger.

"What happened?" I asked, still trying to calm him down.

"We started putting food and water on board yesterday," he said. "They must have noticed what we were doing. Anyway, this morning they put a police guard on the boat and seized all the food."

I'd never had much faith in the boat plan, anyway. Half the refugees in Marseilles knew about it days before the police woke up to it. But now that they had learned about it, too, and had seized the boat, there was sure to be an official inquiry. And that inquiry might lead anywhere. Bohn had good reason to be scared. So did I.

Though I didn't have anything to do with Bohn's boat, I knew the police would think I had, and if he were arrested, I probably would be, too. But my fear took a different form from Bohn's. Instead of shouting, as Bohn was doing, I talked so low he couldn't make out half of what I was saying. This made him more annoyed and nervous than ever, and he suddenly turned and left my room without either one of us having decided what to do.

The failure of the boat plan made no difference to most of the refugees, although it did leave men like Breitscheid and Hilferding stranded. But these men were Bohn's problem. I had problems of my own. I'd planned to put two of my most important refugees on the boat — Franz Werfel and Heinrich

Mann. Both were famous men who would very likely be recognized at the French border. Or if not there, in Spain.

Bohn's boat had seemed the only solution to the problem of getting them out of Europe. Now that solution was no longer available. I had to find some other way.

But I couldn't think of a single one.

11
I Plan the Escape

The next day I came up with an answer. I would be the next guide to the frontier; in fact, I'd travel the whole escape route to Lisbon. And I'd take my two most important refugees, Franz Werfel and Heinrich Mann, with me.

I had been seeing the Franz Werfels every day. Werfel was a well-known writer who had been hiding out in Lourdes before he came to Marseilles. While in Lourdes, he got the idea for his novel, *The Song of Bernadette*, and even now he was working on it.

Werfel, like so many of the refugees, could not get a French exit visa, although, like all the others, he had tried many ways of getting out of France. None of them had been successful, so far. He had even thought of trying to get out of France as a demobilized soldier of the French army. But he was too fat and too soft to pass for a soldier, so I persuaded him to drop this plan.

Now that I had decided to take him with me, the big question still was how to get him out of France. It wasn't his not having an exit visa I was worried about; it was climbing mountains. Without an exit visa, the only way for Werfel to cross the frontier was on foot. Werfel and his wife never so much as went around the block without taking a taxi. In Marseilles, where there were few taxis, they sometimes had to walk, but never for more than a very short distance, and then always on level ground. Could they make it on foot over the Pyrénées Mountains, even though they are lower at the Mediterranean end?

When I saw the Werfels the next day, I asked them if they wanted to try it with me through Spain. I said there might be a chance of getting them across the border on the train, although I couldn't guarantee it. If I couldn't, they would just have to walk. The slim chance of the train, and the knowledge that I would be going, were enough to make them accept immediately.

Then I went to Heinrich Mann and asked him if he and his wife would be willing to try the escape route with us.

He hesitated a moment, and then said, "If you are coming with me, I'll take the chance."

Mann was a brother of the famous German novelist Thomas Mann and an outspoken anti-Nazi — therefore very much wanted by the Gestapo. But I reasoned that if I succeeded with Werfel, I'd succeed with Mann, too. Of course it would have been safer to spread the risk by taking them separately, but time was getting dangerously short, and I couldn't be sure of having another chance to take people through to Lisbon myself. And I didn't want to trust these people to anyone else. They were too prominent, too obviously in danger in Europe. I decided to turn this trip into an all-or-nothing gamble.

There were two other reasons for my wanting to make the trip myself. For one thing, I was supposed to go back to New York. I felt I couldn't leave until someone came over from the States to take my place. Yet I couldn't very well explain the reasons for this to the Committee in a cable or a censored letter from Marseilles. In Lisbon, on the other hand, I could write a long and truthful report of what the real situation was. Then I could go back to Marseilles and wait for the new man to arrive.

My other reason for wanting to make the trip myself was that I wanted to find out why those five refugees had been arrested in Spain. If I knew, perhaps I could see that it didn't happen in the future. Also, I wanted to try to get those who had been arrested out of prison.

In the back of my mind was still another idea. Now that Bohn's boat plan had failed, I wanted to call on the British Embassy in Madrid. I thought maybe I could get the British to help us with Breitscheid, Hilferding, and the other prominent refugees who could not possibly go through Spain, and whose only way out was by sea. If the British could send a small ship from a port outside France to some prearranged point on the coast near Marseilles where we'd have our refugees waiting, a boat could sneak in to shore under the cover of darkness. The refugees could board the ship and be away before the police or the Gestapo had time to hear about it.

All these plans were swimming in my head as I packed to leave for Lisbon. But would they work?

12
The All-or-Nothing Gamble

Early the next morning, we all met at the railroad station: Mr. and Mrs. Franz Werfel, Mr. and Mrs. Heinrich Mann, Golo Mann (Thomas Mann's son, whom Heinrich Mann had asked me to bring along), Dick Ball, and I. Our train left at half past five in the morning. We were excited and nervous. When I suddenly realized the responsibility I was taking on, I became the most nervous and excited one of all. My nervousness and irritability were not reduced by my discovery that the Werfels had brought along twelve suitcases for their desperate escape from death.

We arrived at the frontier town of Cebère just after dark. We got off the train and went into the station, thinking we could go right on out to the street. Then we saw that all the train's passengers were being lined up and made to show their travel documents.

Panic seized me. Except for myself, no one in

our group had a safe-conduct pass or an exit visa. This meant that none of them had the right to be traveling to the border.

But Dick Ball wasn't upset. With all the confidence in the world, he took our passports and went into the office of the frontier police. The rest of us stood about, waiting, talking in low voices and trying to reassure one another.

After a long time, Dick came out of the police office. I could tell from his face that things had not gone well. But when he came up to us, he smiled and said, "Nothing to worry about. Everything's okay."

"But what happened?" we asked him.

"We have to come back tomorrow morning and see if they'll let you go through on the train. Meantime, we can stay at the hotel."

On the way to town, I dropped behind the others and whispered to Dick, "What really happened? Is it bad?"

"I don't like the looks of things," he said. "The *commissaire* was polite enough, but he told me he had strict orders not to let anyone through the border without an exit visa. I argued with him for a while, and he finally agreed to keep the passports and think it over. He'll let us know in the morning. Since the train across the border doesn't leave until two-thirty in the afternoon, we have plenty of time to think. But to be perfectly honest, I think he's going to say no."

The next day dawned clear and hot. We had an early breakfast and sat over coffee while Dick went to get the *commissaire's* answer. When he came back, we could tell from the look on his face what that answer was.

"It's no," he said. "He says he'd do it if he was alone, but there's another *commissaire* on duty with him today, so he doesn't dare."

We all started talking at once. And all of us had the same thought: We're stuck. What do we do now?

"Relax," Dick said. "We'll find a way to work it out."

Then he signaled for me to go outside with him.

As soon as we were outside, he started talking fast.

"Some luck!" he said. "We just hit on a bad day. If that other supervisor wasn't there, he'd have let you all go through on the train. Maybe if you wait around until tomorrow or the next day, he still would. But then again, maybe he wouldn't. It all depends on how long that other one sticks around."

"What do you think we ought to do?" I asked.

"Darned if I know," Dick said. "The *commissaire* says you ought to go over the hill. I told him there was an old man in the party, but he says you ought to risk it anyway. You can't tell what will happen — they might even get an order to arrest the lot of you. He said, 'Tell your friends they'd better get out while they can.' He even came out on the platform and showed me the best trail to take over the hill."

I looked up at the hill. It was pretty high and looked rugged, and the sun was already getting pretty hot.

"Dick," I said, "I don't think Werfel could make it. He's too fat, and Mann's too old. Don't you think I should go back and try to buy false exit visas for the whole lot of them?"

"I don't like the way the *commissaire* talked," Dick said. "He seemed to know something was going to happen. He wasn't kidding when he said to get them out today, while there's still time. If you ask me, I don't think we should hang around here any longer than we have to."

I decided the only thing to do was tell the others the situation. Then it would be up to them to decide what they wanted to do.

When I finished telling them, they looked at one another for a long moment. Then each one nodded. They would go over the hill. Since I had an exit visa, it was agreed that I'd go through on the train with the luggage. We'd all meet on the other side of the border, in the Spanish town of Port-Bou.

We went back to the hotel to pack our overnight bags and check out. Then I made each of them go through their pockets and pocketbooks and make sure they weren't carrying anything that could get them into trouble. When I took Heinrich Mann's hat and began to scratch out his initials on the hatband, he looked at me like a condemned man about to die.

"We have to act like real criminals!" he said.

I walked with them through the village, and as far as the cemetery on the hill. On the way I stopped and bought a dozen packages of cigarettes.

"If you get into any trouble with the frontier

guards," I said, "give them these. It usually works, especially in Spain."

Then I passed the packages of cigarettes out to my five mountain-climbing protégés.

I left them just beyond the cemetery. Half an hour later, I could still see them slowly climbing up across the bare limestone hillside, following the line of stone walls that ran over the hill. They would disappear from sight now and then behind an olive grove, and then I would see them a bit farther up, resting for a moment in the shade of an olive tree.

My train didn't leave until late afternoon, and when it arrived in Port-Bou, I had the bags, all seventeen of them, taken to the hotel. Then I went to the frontier police and asked them if a fat man and stout woman, an elderly man with a slight limp, a middle-aged woman with blonde hair, and a young man with jet-black hair had come through. They said they had seen no such people.

As I paced back and forth on the railroad platform wondering what to do, I got more nervous with every passing minute. Suddenly I remembered a friendly little porter I had talked to in this same station on my way to Marseilles from the States. I found him in the customs office, and when I told him about my problem he said he'd find out right away whether or not my friends had been arrested.

He was back from the police station in about ten minutes. "No," he said. "Nobody's been arrested at Port-Bou today. It's quite unusual, but it appears to be true."

I asked him what he thought I ought to do.

"Why don't you go up to the sentry box at the border post? Maybe they will know something there," he said.

I bought a lot of cigarettes and then headed up the hill. Two tired and hot-looking sentries stood beside the sentry box at the border post. I passed out the cigarettes and then asked, "Have you seen anything of five travelers — three men and two women — coming through on foot?"

They didn't seem to understand me. So I gave them some more cigarettes.

"Look," I said, "I'm worried about some people who came over the hill this morning. Are you sure you haven't seen them?"

"Wait here," one of the sentries said, pointing to a small stool. Then he went into the little house by the gate.

I sat down and nervously started smoking one cigarette after another. I didn't know if I was under arrest or not. In about ten minutes the sentry came back.

"Your friends are at the railroad station," he said. "I just telephoned down. They're waiting for you there."

I don't think I've ever been so relieved in my life as I was by those few words. I gave the sentries all the cigarettes I had left, shook hands with both of them, and started running back down the hill to Port-Bou.

There they were at the station, all five of them, when I came panting up. They were as happy to see me as I was to see them. We fell into one another's arms as though we were old friends who hadn't seen each other in years.

The first and perhaps the most dangerous part of our dash to freedom was over.

But it was still a long way to Lisbon.

13
The Rest
of the Journey

On the way to the hotel in Port-Bou, I heard all about the frontier crossing. It had been a very difficult climb, especially for Heinrich Mann, who was seventy years old. Dick and Golo had had to carry him a good part of the way. Not that Mann wasn't game — he was the gamest of the lot. But he simply couldn't make the steep grade without help.

When they had reached the top of the hill, Dick Ball stopped to get their bearings. Almost immediately, two French frontier guards appeared from out of nowhere and started toward them. It was no use trying to make a run for it. If they did, the guards might shoot at them. So they just stood there, wiping off the sweat of heat and fear and awaiting their fate.

The guards came up to them and saluted, "Are you looking for Spain?" one of them asked.

"Yes," Heinrich Mann said.

"Well," the guard said, "follow the path to the

left. If you take the one to the right, you'll run right into the French border post. And if you haven't got exit visas, you'll be in trouble. The left path will take you right to the Spanish border point. If you report to the sentry box, and don't try to go around it, you'll be all right."

The two guards saluted again, and watched as the group walked single file down the left path.

Ball had walked on with them until they came within sight of the Spanish sentry house. Then he stopped. "Here's where I say good-bye," he said. "You'll make it to Port-Bou okay now." He shook hands with all of them, wished them luck, and turned back toward France.

At the sentry house, there was another scare. The sentries studied each passport very closely. They showed no interest in Mr. and Mrs. Werfel, or in Mr. and Mrs. "Ludwig," the name the Heinrich Manns were traveling under. But one of the sentries showed great interest in Golo Mann. Golo's American visa said he was going to the United States to visit his father, Thomas Mann, at Princeton.

"So, you are the son of Thomas Mann?" the sentry asked.

Visions of Gestapo lists flashed through Golo's mind. He felt this was it. But he decided to play it cool.

"Yes," he said. "Does that displease you?"

"On the contrary," the sentry answered. "I am honored to meet the son of so great a man." And he shook hands warmly with Golo. Then he telephoned down to Port-Bou and had a car sent up from the station. Thus, while I was climbing up the hill, my group was already riding down the same hill in comfort to meet me!

It was all so much like a comic opera that it went to our heads. We drank a great deal of Spanish wine with our late lunch at the hotel. We had all agreed that under no circumstances would we call Mr. and Mrs. Mann by their right names while we were in Spain. Mann was not only an enemy of the German dictatorship of Adolf Hitler, he was also an enemy of the Spanish dictatorship of Generalissimo Francisco Franco. If his name were recognized, the Spanish police would almost certainly arrest him at once and turn him over to the Gestapo.

But the members of my little party of desperate refugees were all so happy about getting over the border, and so hopeful about their approaching delivery from danger in Lisbon, that some of them forgot. They were saying Herr Mann this, and Herr Mann that, Frau Mann this, and Frau Mann that, until all caution was abandoned.

There were several other people in the small dining room, among them the British Consul, whom I had met on my way through Spain in early August. He came up to me and put his hand on my shoulder.

"May I speak to you a moment, old man?" he said.

We went out into the hallway.

"That chap with you is Heinrich Mann, isn't he?" he asked.

"Yes" I said.

"Well," he said, "I'd be a little careful if I were you. You don't know who that bloke in the uniform is, do you?"

I had noticed a man in uniform sitting at a corner table in the dining room, but I hadn't paid much attention to him.

"No," I said. "I have no idea. Who is he?"

"He happens to be the head of the Spanish Secret Police in this area," the British Consul said. "He's not a very pleasant chap, really. I'd be a bit more careful, if I were you."

I thanked him warmly for the tip. Then I went back to the table. As quietly as I could, I told Golo what the British Consul had just told me. Golo whispered in German to Mrs. Werfel, and she whispered to her husband. All of us fell silent. A few minutes later, we all went up to our rooms.

The next day, our group went from Port-Bou to Barcelona by train. We planned to fly to Lisbon from there. But in Barcelona I found there were no seats on the Lisbon plane until Monday, and even then there would be only two places available. I decided to buy the two seats on the Monday plane and give them to Mr. and Mrs. Mann, who were in greater danger in Spain than any of the rest of us.

We stayed in Barcelona over the weekend. Then, early Monday morning, Golo and I went with Heinrich Mann and his wife to the office of the Spanish airline, where Mr. and Mrs. Mann were to take a bus to the airport.

When Mann saw a portrait of Adolf Hitler on the office wall, he nearly lost his nerve.

"We are in the hands of the enemy," he said solemnly.

We got him a brandy to revive his courage and then rode to the airport with him. As I watched the plane taxi down the runway, I thought: Well, the Manns, at last, are safely off to Lisbon.

The Werfels, Golo, and I took the noon train to Madrid. At the airline office there, I was lucky. I got two cancellations for that same afternoon. They went, of course, to the Werfels.

At the airport, I had the same thought as with the Manns: Well, the Werfels, at last, are safely off to Lisbon.

Back from the airport, I met Golo Mann, who had spent the day at the Prado Museum. I got him on a train for Lisbon that same night. I breathed a great sigh of relief. All my protégés were now safely on their way.

That left me free to get back to other business. Before I left Madrid, I wanted to see what I could do about the refugees who had been arrested and were now prisoners in a Spanish jail.

Early the next day, I went to see the State Security Police to inquire about them. I spent all morning being shunted from one official to the next. But, finally, I got the promise of a report on my people when I returned to Madrid on my way back to Marseilles. That afternoon I boarded a plane. I, too, at last, was safely off to Lisbon.

On arrival, I went right from the airport to the Hotel Metropole. Franzi von Hildebrand, who, with his family, had come through from Marseilles a week or so before, was waiting for me.

"You have a telegram from Marseilles," he said, handing me an envelope. I tore it open and we read the brief message together.

BABY PASSED CRISIS. BETTER NOW. BUT OTHER CHILDREN QUARANTINED. DOING OUR BEST. LENA.

"What the devil is that all about?" Franzi asked.

"I think it means all our refugees in Marseilles have been arrested and sent to concentration camps, except Mehring," I said. Then I read the telegram again. "Or maybe it means they've all been confined to their hotels by the police. To tell you the truth, Franzi, I'm not sure what it means. But I do know one thing. I've got to get back to Marseilles as soon as possible."

That night I had dinner with the Manns. Then, the next morning, I visited the Werfels. In the afternoon, I wrote a long report to the Committee in New York, telling them exactly how things were in France. The rest of my time in Lisbon I spent interviewing the many refugees I had sent through from France who were still in Portugal.

The refugees' tales of what had happened at the French frontier were as many and varied as the people who had crossed it. Some had gone through on the train, even though they had no exit visas. Others had had to walk over the Pyrénées. Some were stopped by the French border guards and sent back. Others were directed to the Spanish border posts, just as the Werfels and the Manns had been. One German refugee had not been allowed to leave France until he had sworn his passport was false. When he gave his word it was, he was allowed to go through without any further questioning. Another German refugee, who crossed after I did, and who passed me in Spain, had found German agents at the French border the day after the Werfels and Manns had climbed over the hill. He and his wife had to climb by a much more roundabout route, which meant they had to spend the night in the mountains. I was glad we'd followed the *commissaire's* advice and gotten out of there the same day! Otherwise, the Werfels and Manns might not have reached Lisbon.

The refugees' stories of what had happened on the trip through Spain were equally varied. Some had had difficulty at the Spanish frontier. Some said their baggage had been thoroughly searched. Some even had to go into a little room at the railway station at Port-Bou and undress to show the Spanish police that they weren't smuggling money into Spain. Others had no trouble of any sort. Almost all of them said that the passport examinations on the trains between the border and the frontier of Portugal were very thorough. Those with false passports had been scared almost out of their wits.

But to most of the refugees, the worst thing about the whole trip was the fleas in the third-class railway carriages.

The many and varied stories confused me. A great deal seemed to depend on luck. But we had little choice of escape routes. For the present, at least, the one we were using seemed to be the best and the safest, and it seemed wise to continue using it. When I got back to Marseilles, I would try harder than ever to persuade the refugees still left there to take this route before it was too late.

I was ready to start back to Marseilles. But there was one last thing I had to do before leaving Lisbon. It was the most vital errand of my whole trip: I had to buy some soap.

Because of the soap shortage in France, Lena had tucked little notes in every part of my baggage as reminders to bring soap back with me. She had written these notes in every language she knew. When I opened my shaving kit, a piece of paper fell out with the word *savon* written on it. When I put on a clean shirt, another piece of paper fluttered to the floor. It read *sapone*. Between the handkerchiefs in my suitcase was a note reading *seife*. In the toe of a clean pair of socks I found a slip saying *jabon*. In still other places I found the same reminder in English, Polish, and Russian.

If I arrived back in Marseilles without soap, I'd have worse than the Gestapo to face. So I told the salesgirl, "Three dozen of the biggest cakes of your best soap, please."

14
I Become
a British Agent

Back in Madrid, where I'd been only four days before, I checked into the Hotel Nacional. After getting a few papers from my overnight case, I went straight to the British Embassy. They were expecting me, although not quite as soon as this. Four days ago, just before taking the plane to Lisbon, I had stopped in at the Embassy. Since Bohn's escape-ship plan had failed, I wanted to find out if the British could send a ship and sea-rescue those of my refugees who could not escape through Spain.

Major Torr, the Military Attaché who had received me on that first visit, had been most helpful and cooperative. Before he talked to me, he leaned down and pulled the telephone wire out of a plug in the floor beside his chair.

"You have to be most careful," he said. "They can use these things as listening devices, you know. Even when the receiver is down."

"I didn't know," I said. "But I'm glad to find out.

When I get back from Lisbon, I'll have our office phones changed."

Then I told Major Torr what I had come to see him about.

"I'm afraid the Embassy can do nothing 'officially,'" he said. "We had the same idea of sending a boat to rescue our soldiers caught by the German occupation. But the Navy has a strict rule never to take a ship away from the fleet for such a purpose. So I'm afraid we'll have to work out another scheme. Perhaps something 'unofficial.'"

Just then the phone rang. Major Torr plugged it back in and picked up the receiver. When he had finished, he was careful to unplug it again.

"That was the head of the Spanish Secret Police," he said. "For weeks I've been seeking his cooperation in getting our men who cross the French frontier out of Spain to Gibraltar. If he goes along with us, there is only one other person we need. That one person is vital to the success of our plan." He smiled warmly and leaned toward me. "You've come at the right moment. That one person could be you!"

"Me?" I said, surprised.

"You," he repeated. "To carry out our plan, we must have an agent in France. Someone to round up our boys and get them across the French border. You know the situation there. You are the logical man for us."

"But I have my own people to take care of," I said. "That's why I've come to see you. I want your help with my people."

"Perhaps we can kill two birds with one stone," he said. "You help us with our soldiers; we'll help you with your refugees."

"How would we work it?" I asked.

"Tell you what," he said. "You're now on your way to Lisbon, but you'll be back in Madrid in a week or so. Could you come in to see me then? Meantime, I'll talk it over with His Excellency, the Ambassador. Also, it will give me a chance to get some definite answers from the head of the Secret Police. Then we can plan more intelligently."

Now, here I was back in Madrid. Only, instead of a week, just four days had passed. But so many things were happening so fast, each day, each hour, was vital.

At the Embassy, Major Torr received me immediately. "I didn't expect you quite so soon," he said.

I explained about the telegram from Lena and my uncertainty about what was happening in Marseilles.

"It's just as well," Major Torr said, "I expect our time is getting short."

He plugged in his telephone and asked to be connected with the Ambassador. When he had finished talking, he pulled the plug out again.

"His Excellency will see us right away," he said.

We went down to the Ambassador's room. The Ambassador, a much older man than I had expected, was just finishing his tea.

"Major Torr tells me you're willing to help us get our men out of France," the Ambassador said.

"I'll certainly be glad to try," I said.

"Major Torr has made an arrangement with the Spanish authorities. They will release any of our men who cross the frontier from France into Spain on the grounds that they are escaping prisoners of war. Do you think you can get our men across the frontier?"

I said I thought it was possible. Then I explained that though I was willing to help the British get their soldiers out of France, my main concern was still with my political refugees who couldn't enter Spain because of their activities during the Spanish Civil War.

"I see," the Ambassador said. "You must have a ship for these refugees of yours, is that it?"

I said it was.

"Well," he said, "I am willing to place $10,000 at your disposal. Would you be willing to spend part of this money to get our men across the frontier? And, with the rest of it, would you be willing to hire boats and organize escapes by sea? If you are successful, you could send some of our men out by sea along with your refugees."

I hadn't figured on anything like this. It would make me a British secret agent, and I didn't like that idea. It might prove very dangerous. France and Britain had already broken diplomatic relations and might be at war with one another any day. And even if they weren't, the Gestapo would be much more interested in my activities as a British agent than they were in my activities as an individual rescuing political refugees.

But I needed the help of the British if I was to get my people out, so I decided to make a bargain. I told the Ambassador I would organize the escapes if, at the same time, he would undertake to hire Spanish ships to go to the French coast and pick up the refugees and the British soldiers I would have waiting there.

The Ambassador turned to Major Torr. "What do you think, Torr?" he said.

Torr said he thought it would be possible to get some Spanish fishing boats to go up from Barcelona to the coast of France.

"Very well, then," the Ambassador said. "It's agreed. We'll arrange to send fishing boats. You'll arrange to have your refugees and our soldiers ready to leave on these boats."

"Agreed," I said.

"Now I'll leave you to work out the details with Major Torr."

We shook hands, then Torr and I went back to Torr's office.

I asked to have the $10,000 paid to the Committee in New York. Then through Dimitru I could pick up French francs in Marseilles as I needed them. Torr and I also worked out a code with which to keep in touch with one another.

The next afternoon, I took a plane from Madrid to Barcelona. I went immediately to the American Consulate to find out if there was any word about the five refugees who had been jailed. The Consulate had the news I was looking for. All five prisoners had been charged with secret entry into Spain and with smuggling. Evidently they had not presented themselves at the first border post, but had gone deep into Spain without getting entrance stamps on their passports. The Consulate thought my refugees had not been arrested because of past political activities in Germany, but simply on border technicalities.

I went at once to see a lawyer. He was very hopeful about getting the prisoners out of jail. He said he would go to work on it at once and keep me informed of his progress. Since there was nothing more I could do here, I left at once for the frontier.

15
Back in Marseilles

There was an ominous gray sky over Marseilles when I came out of the station. The mistral, that cold, dry north wind that blows over the Mediterranean coast of France, was blowing the first dried leaves of autumn off the plane trees and sending them hurtling across the square.

Lena and Beamish met me, and we all went to the Hotel Splendide and had breakfast together. Instead of sugar for our coffee, as we'd had a month before, the waiter brought us saccharine tablets. And instead of cherries and syrup, we now had a brown sticky gelatin made from grapes after the wine had been pressed from them. It was gluey and tasted bitter. There was no butter, and the bread was stale. A new ruling prohibited the eating of fresh bread. The coffee consisted mostly of burned grain.

After breakfast, I unpacked and distributed the

cakes of soap I'd brought from Lisbon. Lena's eyes filled with joy.

"Oh, Mr. Fry," she said. *"Il ne faut pas exagérer."* Beamish and I both laughed.

Then Beamish and Lena told me what had happened while I was away.

I had misunderstood Lena's telegram. It wasn't true, as I had thought, that all the refugees in France had been arrested and placed in forced residence or interned in camps. The day after I had left Marseilles, the National Police had come to pick up the two Rudolfs: Breitscheid and Hilferding. Since it was a simple arrest, neither man was frightened enough to take the poison he carried in his vest pocket. The police also picked up another refugee named Arthur Wolff. Then they came to the hotel to get Walter Mehring. But since Baby was supposed to be ill, and had a doctor's certificate to prove it, he refused to budge from the Splendide. After a battle, in which Lena played the star role, the police had gone away without arresting Baby. He was still safe in his sick room at the hotel.

Breitscheid, Hilferding, and Wolff, under orders from Vichy, were taken to the town of Arles. There they were put under house arrest and kept in a hotel where the police could keep an eye on them. Now they were where the Gestapo could pick them up at any time they wished to do so.

This was not all that had happened. While I was away, the Chief of the National Police had called the American Consul to come to his office. He told the Consul that Vichy was most "uneasy" about the "activities of Dr. Bohn and Mr. Fry." He requested that the Consul-General of the American Consulate take some immediate action in regard to both of us.

I was not at all sure what would happen now, or just what I should do. Lena and Beamish felt that, no matter what, I had to stay in France. Without an American to protect them, they said, everyone in the office would soon be arrested and sent to a concentration camp. Everything we were trying to do for the refugees would come to an end.

And our work was by no means finished. We hadn't sent out everyone we had located even weeks before. And each day we were finding more and more of the refugees on my lists. Somehow we had to find a way to get all these people out of France.

16
The Door Swings Shut

Everything happened so fast in the next few days, it seems it all happened at once.

I had our office telephone changed. I told the telephone company we wanted to be able to move the phone around from room to room. Men came and put an outlet in each room and installed a plug on the instrument cord. Now, like the British in Madrid, we could unplug the phone when we were not using it. In my room at the Splendide, where we could not have a plug installed, we put a hat over the phone when it was not in use. Even with these precautions, we inspected both the office and the hotel room every day for signs of a hidden microphone.

Next I went to the American Consulate to see the Consul-General. He advised me to leave France at once, before I was arrested or expelled. He wouldn't tell me what the Chief of the National Police had said, nor would he show me a copy of the report on me he had cabled to the State Department in Washington. But he did show me the State Department's reply. The reply contained the definite statement that:

"THIS GOVERNMENT CANNOT COUNTENANCE THE ACTIVITIES REPORTED OF DR. BOHN AND MR. FRY AND OTHER PERSONS IN THEIR EFFORTS IN EVADING THE LAWS OF COUNTRIES WITH WHICH THE UNITED STATES MAINTAINS FRIENDLY RELATIONS."

I telegraphed the American Embassy at Vichy and asked it not to take any action on cancelling my passport until I had a chance to come to Vichy to see them. The only answer I got was a message by telephone from the Embassy in Vichy to the Consulate in Marseilles saying there was no use in my coming to Vichy: A report had been sent to the State Department in Washington over a week ago with all the information. No other action for or against me was contemplated at this time.

I decided to go to Vichy anyway. But I found I couldn't get a safe-conduct pass to travel unless the Consulate or the Embassy requested it from the police, and neither of them would do so. I then asked the Consul to cable my side of the story to the State Department. He refused to do so on the grounds that my case had already been judged and nothing I could add would now make any difference.

During this time of telegrams and cables and telephone calls and meetings, I was also trying to make every minute count for the refugees. But luck was against me. Although we did get a lot of people out of France in those last days of September, we also had a lot of disappointments and disasters.

Our next big problem came from Portugal, which quite suddenly changed its visa rules. The Portuguese Consul became very strict about issuing transit visas for crossing through Portugal to Lisbon. He would issue transit visas only on certain passports and foreign visas. This made practically all of our false passports and visas worthless as travel documents.

I had been back in Marseilles only a few days when someone brought me word that Georg Bernhard, one of the three men Barellet had told me the Gestapo was looking for, was still in France. Bernhard and his wife were staying in the town of Narbonne. I sent Dick Ball down to Narbonne immediately to get the Bernhards and bring them back to Marseilles. I wanted to get them across the frontier and to Lisbon before the Gestapo got wind of their whereabouts.

When Dick returned to Marseilles with the Bernhards, we hid them in one of the tourist hotels. The proprietor of the hotel thought they were an amorous — if somewhat overage — couple who were having a secret romance, and so he overlooked the formality of reporting their presence to the police, as he was supposed to do with all hotel guests.

The Bernhards had American visas waiting for them at the Consulate, and we were planning to buy them false passports for their safe travel to

Lisbon. Now, with the new ruling from Portugal, this would no longer work. Also, we were still trying to get Baby out of Marseilles. We did not want to risk sending him through Spain under his own name, nor did we want him to travel in France without a safe-conduct pass. We decided to buy him a Lithuanian passport under an assumed name and try to get him a safe-conduct permit to some town near the Spanish border. The only problem was a photograph for the passport. Baby could not leave his sick room because of the police, and it would be too obvious to have a photographer come to the hotel. Finally, we found a refugee photographer we could trust to do the job. We were all set now and had only to get Baby his transit visas, and he would be safely off to Lisbon.

Then Spain closed off its entire frontier.

17
Escape by Sea

I remember well that terrible day. I went down to the office as usual, but I could tell from the hum of excited conversation as I entered the waiting room that something was wrong. At first I thought it was another raid by the police picking up refugees. As I tried to work my way through the crowd, the refugees seized me by the sleeves and asked if I'd heard the news. The Spanish frontier was closed.

It looked like the end. Now the refugees were really trapped. They were to be kept in France as cattle are kept in the pens of a slaughterhouse, and the Gestapo had only to come and get them. There would be no more escapes.

It turned out to be not quite so bad as it seemed that first day. But there was panic among the refugees for several weeks. During this time the Spaniards opened and closed their frontier again and again. Sometimes it would be open for only a few hours, and sometimes for a whole day. We never could tell in advance, and we never knew, when the frontier closed, if it would ever open again. It was a cruel way to torture human beings. Every opening of the frontier meant hope renewed, every closing — hope abandoned.

The Portuguese changed their rulings regarding travel documents. So did the Spanish. Then both countries changed them again.

With so many changes of rulings, it was almost impossible to get all the necessary travel documents ready at the same time. By the time one permit or visa was ready, another would have expired, or the ruling would have changed, and one document or another would be invalid. Very often by the time we got the refugees a Spanish visa, their Portuguese visa had expired, and we would have to start all over again. Once all their travel papers were in order, the ship that was to carry them to America had left Lisbon without them. For some time to come, the only people who were able to leave France were those who already had both Spanish and Portuguese visas in their passports before the end of September, when the new rulings had started flying back and forth.

The Consul-General kept telling me I'd be expelled from France any day — if I were lucky enough not to be arrested and held on charges.

But there were four friends of Paul Hagen, the German underground leader I'd met in New York, who were being held in the prison camp at Vernet. Paul had particularly asked me to help these men, and I did not want to leave Marseilles until I had gotten them out of France.

The first step, of course, was to get them out of Vernet. We had sent letters and telegrams to the commandant in the name of the Committee, but to no avail. There were only two things left to try: escape and feminine wiles.

Escape was practically impossible. Vernet was more closely guarded than any other concentration camp in France. It was surrounded by a high barbed-wire fence, and the section where Paul's friends were held had a second barbed-wire fence inside the first. The guards were old soldiers, armed with rifles, who were held personally responsible for all escapes and their instructions were to shoot to kill.

Feminine wiles seemed safer. For this we had a made-to-order charmer in the person of Mary Jayne Gold. Mary Jayne was young, blonde, and beautiful. Before the Germans had arrived, she had had a large apartment in Paris and her own low-wing monoplane, in which she used to toot around Europe. She would fly to Switzerland for the skiing and to the Italian Riviera for the sun. When war broke out, she gave her plane to the French government. It would be hard to find a better person for the job we had in mind than Mary Jayne.

Mary Jayne said she would try her best. She went to Vernet, saw the commandant, and succeeded where everybody else had failed. Accompanied by two soldier guards, the four prisoners were allowed to come to Marseilles to get their American visas. When they had them, they were supposed to go back to the camp, still under guard. But Beamish and I had other plans. We had arranged to send the four men through Spain, hoping that by the time the guards realized what had happened and had given the alarm, their prisoners would already be in Lisbon.

Everything worked all right, up to a point. The four men came to Marseilles, went to the American Consulate, and got their American visas. But before we could get them Portuguese and Spanish transit visas, the Spanish frontier was closed. We had to find some other way to smuggle them out of France. And at once. Otherwise they would go back to Vernet, and what would happen to them there we couldn't know.

By great good luck, Beamish had found a boat — the *Bouline*. Some young Frenchmen who wanted to join the Resistance had bought the *Bouline* and planned to sail her to Gibraltar.

Luckily, the guards of the four prisoners from Vernet liked liquor and women. Given the money, they could easily be persuaded to spend the night on the town. They were too drunk to know much of anything on the night the *Bouline* sailed for Gibraltar with Paul Hagen's four friends aboard.

When Beamish came to my room at the Splendide about two o'clock in the morning and reported that the boat had actually left port and headed out to sea, I had the same feelings a man must have who has just murdered a hated rival. Paul's friends had

*Varian Fry in his office in Marseilles, probably
Boulevard Garibaldi. (Photo by Lipnitzki. No date.)*

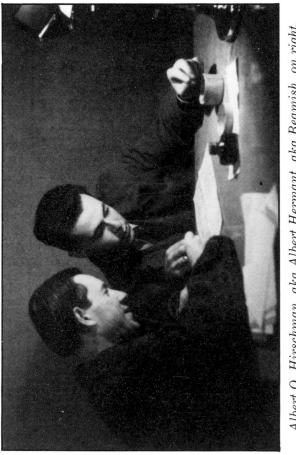

*Albert O. Hirschman, aka Albert Hermant, aka Beamish, on right,
with unidentified man. Centre Américain de Secours office, Rue Grignan.
(Photographer unknown. No date.)*

View of the port of Marseilles, possibly from Varian Fry's hotel room window.
(Photo by Varian Fry. No date.)

Jacqueline Breton, André Masson, André Breton, and Varian Fry in Fry's office at the American Relief Center, Boulevard Garibaldi, Marseilles. (Photo by Ylla. February 1941.)

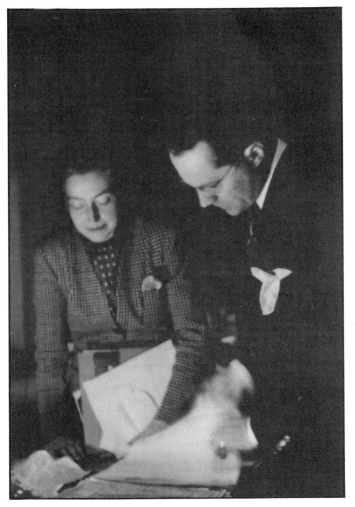

Miriam Davenport and Varian Fry.
(Photographer unknown. No date.)

Daniel Bénédite, presumably in Marseilles. (Photo by Varian Fry. 1941.)

View of Cerbère with the wall of the railway station. From the front of a postcard sent by Varian Fry to his mother in August 1940.

*Marc Chagall standing in front of his painting
"Three Candles." (Photographer unknown. 1940–41.)*

gotten away. But how could we hope to escape being implicated? When the guards sobered up in the morning and discovered their prisoners had disappeared, they would certainly go to the police. The police would make an investigation, and the finger of guilt would point directly to us.

How would we get out of this one?

18
Failure

Four or five days later, Dick Ball brought us the news. He had just come up from Narbonne. As he got off the train, he had seen Paul Hagen's four friends chained together and heavily guarded, waiting on another platform. We wouldn't believe him at first, but he insisted there could be no mistake about it. We got our Corsican lawyer to make inquiries and we soon learned that Dick had been right.

The *Bouline* had slipped out of port right under the noses of the port guard. She had sailed all that night and all the next day. Then, toward evening, she had run into a storm. The wind tore the sails; the waves lashed the deck. By nightfall, the little boat was out of control and leaking badly. Half the passengers were so seasick they didn't care whether they lived or died. The others worked the pump till it broke. Then they bailed out with pails.

Toward morning the storm subsided, and the day

dawned calm and clear. Paul's friends wanted to continue the trip at all costs, if not to Gibraltar, then to Spain or Corsica. But everyone else on board had had enough. They ignored the pleas of the prisoners and the consequences to themselves if they returned to Marseilles. At about half past eight in the morning, they brought the boat around and started back toward the same port they had left.

Toward noon, a French coast-guard vessel overtook them and towed them to the little harbor of Port de Bouc. There they were arrested and sent to Aix-en-Provence to await trial on charges of attempting to leave France without authorization. It was while they were being transferred from the train to the Aix-en-Provence trolley that Dick had seen them.

We hired a battery of lawyers to defend them, and expected, at any moment, to have to hire another battery of lawyers to defend ourselves. But after three months in jail, awaiting trial, the four men were sentenced to one month in prison. Because they had already served three times that long, they were immediately set free. As they walked out of the courtroom, the Vichy government was waiting to pick them up. They were all returned to the prison of Vernet, where they were put under a much heavier guard.

Our connection with the attempted escape, and the *Bouline*, was never mentioned. If the police were suspicious, they did not reveal it.

During all this time, Frank Bohn and I were called to the American Consulate almost every day and asked when we were planning to leave France. We also got cables from our relatives and friends and employers in the United States urging us to come home.

Bohn finally decided to go and left the first week in October. I stayed. With Mehring in bed, the Bernhards still waiting in the tourist hotel, and Paul's friends still in prison, I felt more than ever that I couldn't leave now, no matter what pressures were brought to bear on me.

There was another reason for my decision to stay. Charlie Fawcett had a friend in the American Ambulance Service whose cousin was in the German Army. This cousin asked a German officer friend to call on Charlie's friend in Marseilles. Among the things they talked about was me.

"Sure, we know all about Fry," the German officer had said. "We know he's trying to get our political enemies out of France. We aren't worrying. We're confident he won't succeed."

This challenge was too difficult to ignore. I determined to prove them wrong.

The night before Frank Bohn left Marseilles, he asked me to take over his work in France in conjunction with my own. I agreed. Now, in addition to the intellectuals, the Catholics, the younger socialists, and the British soldiers, I also had the responsibility for Breitscheid, Hilferding, and all the other older leaders of the various labor and socialist movements of Europe.

There would be only one man for the Gestapo agents to keep their eye on. Me.

19
Reorganizing
Our Office

Heinrich Himmler, the Gestapo chief, was being feted in Madrid. We weren't sure what his visit meant, but we could guess. Gestapo agents were on the French side of the frontier, and the Spanish border had been closed. A new regulation had been issued whereby the names of all visa applicants must be telegraphed to Madrid before travel visas through Spain could be granted. All this could mean only one thing. Berlin was at last giving serious attention to the refugees in France.

For some reason, the Gestapo had allowed us more than six weeks to get our refugees out. We didn't know why, but we were grateful for the time and we had profited by it. Now we knew our days of grace were over. With each passing day it became more urgent to act quickly. Though obviously against her will, France was slowly and steadily bowing to the will of Hitler's "New Order."

Early in September it was decreed that the heads

of police bureaus should have the right to intern, without trial, anyone who was thought to be "dangerous to public safety."

At the beginning of October, it was announced that foreigners between the ages of eighteen and fifty-five might be formed into forced-labor gangs. These men would receive no wages for their work, but their families could draw relief.

A few days before Himmler's visit to Madrid, the French adopted their first anti-Jewish law, barring all French Jews from holding public office and from being employed in the teaching profession, journalism, motion pictures, and radio. The new law also gave the police heads the right to arrest all foreign Jews and intern them in concentration camps or place them under house arrest. Late in October, Vichy adopted a law forbidding people to listen to English radio broadcasts. And rumors were constantly repeated that the Nazis were going to occupy the so-called "free zone."

About this time, Marshal Pétain met with Hitler. After the meeting, the policy of collaboration between France and Germany was announced. Did this mean the French police and the Gestapo would work more closely together? The French police suddenly became more active in late October. There was a series of raids, and many refugees were picked up and sent off to concentration camps. Among those picked up were a good number of our own protégés.

But more than anything else, it was the Kundt Commission that made us feel that we had to hurry if we were to save any more of the refugees who were in danger.

The Kundt Commission was a group of German army officers and Gestapo agents who visited the French concentration camps looking for those men the Gestapo wanted sent back to Germany under Article 19 — the Surrender on Demand article — of the armistice.

All these new developments had two consequences for us. First, we would have to reorganize our work. Whereas we had been hoping to finish up in a few weeks, we would now have to plan for a long haul. Second, we would have to support many of the refugees and try to keep them out of jails or concentration camps. Instead of a half-transparent cover for our illegal operations, we would turn the office into a genuine relief organization, staffed by professional relief workers who would have no idea at all that we were doing any underground work.

So as the original workers left, I replaced them with new people who knew nothing about the real purpose of my mission to France. In this way, if the police questioned them, they could easily deny that any illegal activities were going on. I wanted to divorce the underground work from the office altogether.

When at last Lena left for the frontier, I replaced her with a new secretary named Mrs. Anna Gruss. Mrs. Gruss was a little gnome of a woman, about four and a half feet tall. She had a good heart and a sharp tongue. She was a tireless worker, and best of all, she was genuinely innocent of our undercover work. If Mrs. Gruss knew what we were doing, she never let on.

Another new person, Daniel Bénédite, had worked in the police bureau in Paris. He was slight and dark and wore a small mustache. In his job, he had had much to do wih refugees. He was friendly with many of them because of his kindness and readiness to help them. Danny became my office chief, taking my place whenever I was too busy to see someone myself. He also performed a hundred other tasks ably and cheerfully.

When I hired Danny, I told him the job would only be for two or three weeks. I didn't believe the police would let us stay open any longer than that. As it turned out, Danny's job lasted for four years. He advanced to leader of the underground network that rescued many of the refugees and kept many others in hiding after the Germans occupied the whole of France.

Another new office member was Danny's war comrade, Jean Gemahling, a blue-eyed, flaxen-haired youth from Strasbourg. He would have been extremely handsome except that his nose was a trifle too long for his face. Jean had been educated at an English boarding school and spoke excellent English, though with a slight French accent. He was very quiet, and usually blushed furiously when spoken to. In the course of time, however, Jean showed a courage and a devotion to duty that many far rougher men would have found difficult to match.

At Walter Mehring's suggestion, I also hired Marcel Chaminade. Baby recommended Chaminade because of his far-reaching connections. Chaminade knew many members of the aristocracy and the upper classes and he could get through doors that might otherwise have been closed to us. Chaminade was not very prepossessing in appearance. Short, bald, and with big protruding ears, he looked and acted like something left over from the court of Napoleon III. When I first met him, he bowed so low I thought for one horrible instant he was going to kiss my hand. He was lazy, loved luxury, and gave the impression of a man who had learned to sleep through life with a minimum of effort. But he was genuinely concerned about the refugees, perhaps because some of them were his old friends from Berlin and Paris.

Chaminade became our ambassador to the French authorities. He performed his duties faithfully, if in a rather show-off manner, for many months to come. We never took Chaminade into our inner circle, and I don't think he ever knew more about our clandestine activities than he could pick up from wisps of conversation. Beamish distrusted and hated him, and Danny Bénédite became very suspicious of him.

With our new office staff, most of whom were French, and all of whom were professionally qualified in one way or another, our relief office took on a much more normal appearance. For the first time, we could present a really respectable face to the authorities.

An ever-increasing number of refugees came to the office every day. Most of them were flat broke.

There were writers who could no longer collect their royalties or get their manuscripts to their publishers, painters who could find no market for their pictures, and professors who had had to leave their jobs at the French universities and were no longer drawing their salaries. There were scientists who had been driven from their laboratories by the Nazi invaders. All of them would have gone hungry or been interned in camps if we had not helped them. By giving them small weekly allowances, we could keep at least some of them out of the camps. To those who were in the camps we could and did send small weekly food parcels. Our relief program was no longer an excuse for being. It was now the principal part of our work.

We hoped the police and the Gestapo were not watching us quite so closely.

But we were never sure.

20
The Search

For the first time since my arrival in France, I was able to take an occasional Sunday off. I still began work at eight o'clock every morning and remained until eleven at night, and sometimes until one. I still saw dozens of people every day, and I was witness to displays of every possible quality of character, from heroic to despicable. Poor, driven refugees still pursued me in the morning when I went out and in the evening when I came in. I still had six to twelve phone calls an hour and got dozens of letters a day. But the pressure slackened, not because the situation was improving, but because more and more of our refugees were being arrested and interned, and there was little or nothing we could do about it.

I took advantage of the slight letup to see something of southern France and get a little rest. One Monday, after my return from a weekend excursion to the country, the telephone rang. It was Mrs. Gruss.

"Wait there," she said. "I'll be right over. Don't come to the office till I've seen you. It's important."

She arrived a few minutes later, as gnomelike as ever.

"The police have been looking for you all morning," she said. "They have an order to search the office and your room. But they couldn't do it without you."

"What are they looking for?" I asked.

"It's funny," she said. "They're looking for false passports. What would you be doing with false passports?"

"What do you think I'd better do?" I asked.

"I guess you'd better go down to headquarters and tell them you're here," she said.

"All right," I said. "But I want to see Beamish first. Can you find him and send him right over?"

"Okay," she said.

"Send Chaminade over too, if he's there," I said.

"Okay."

As soon as she had gone, I took my maps of the frontier from behind the mirror and burned them. I went through all my other papers and burned many of them, too.

Beamish arrived a half hour later.

"Where the devil were you?" I asked.

"What do you mean?" he said.

"*Toujours dans la lune*," I said. "Didn't you remember those maps of the frontier?"

"Yes."

"Suppose the police had found them?"

He shrugged. "Everything's okay. It was a break your being late. Gave me time to clean things up," he said.

"Are you sure everything's okay?" I asked.

"Absolutely," he said. "Just go tell the police you're back. Let them search. They won't find anything. After they search the place maybe they won't be so suspicious."

Chaminade came in a few minutes later and went to Police Headquarters with me. He was magnificent there. He introduced himself as a former French consul. He made a little speech about the American who had "risked so much" to come to France and "help her in her darkest hour." Then he said I had an appointment with the Bishop at five o'clock — a complete lie — and asked them to hurry up with their search if they had to make it so that I would not be late.

I don't know if it was Chaminade's speech or the natural sympathy of the French for Americans, but they made the most superficial search possible. We went around to the office in a police car. They looked in a few drawers and cupboards. Then they made out a form that said they had searched the premises thoroughly and had found nothing suspicious. They signed it, and I signed it. Then we all shook hands, and they went away.

After the police had gone, Beamish and I made a little search of our own. In the stove in the waiting room we found several false identity cards. Were they a plant? Or had someone unloaded them there when the police came in to look for me that morning?

We didn't know.

But I gave Charlie instructions to burn all the papers in the stove every day after that.

21
The Ship That Didn't Sail

During most of October, Beamish and I investigated escape routes by sea. We must have checked at least twenty different boat schemes during that time.

In New York, it had been easy to talk about sending the refugees to Casablanca or Gibraltar by ship. All one had to do was open an atlas and trace a line on a map. But in Marseilles it was a different story altogether. There were only yachts and fishing boats in the harbor and all yachts were forbidden to leave their moorings. The fishing boats all belonged to Marseilles types who were either gangsters or should have been.

Again and again we were told stories about fully equipped vessels ready to slip away from port in the dead of night. But when we checked, we found these boats, offered us for a high price, were gaunt hulks whose bare ribs were held upright only by the support of the sand in which they had been firmly embedded for twenty years. Sometimes it was a phantom ship that didn't exist at all, and never had.

I had gotten in touch with the British as soon as I returned from my trip to Lisbon, contacting two young Englishmen named Graham and Lloyd whom I had run into when I first came to Marseilles. They introduced me to an English officer, a young, blond, and pink-cheeked captain of a Northumberland Regiment named Fitch. Despite his youth, Fitch was the highest-ranking British officer available. He was in charge of evacuating the more than three hundred British soldiers who had been caught by the German occupation.

These soldiers were being held at Fort St. Jean, one of the two old forts that guard the entrance to Marseilles's Old Port. Though they were interned at the fort, the soldiers were allowed to go out into the town during the day. Thus it was an easy matter to send them down to the frontier in twos and threes.

I told Fitch all I knew about routes over the border. Also, from time to time, I gave him money from the $10,000 the British Ambassador had given me in Madrid.

To take the places of the soldiers from the fort who were escaping across the frontier, Fitch substituted civilians from the British Seamen's Institute. The French officer in charge of the fort merely counted noses every morning. If there was always the same number of men in the fort, he was satisfied. In this way, Fitch got many highly skilled men, pilots, and specialists out of France.

Fitch wasn't much interested in boats as long as he could get his men out through Spain. But toward the end of October, Dr. Charles Joy came through from Lisbon. The train on which he traveled was so crowded Dr. Joy had had to stand up in the toilet for most of the way, along with four women and a potted chrysanthemum. Not only was he tired from the trip, but he was also exhausted emotionally by this unaccustomed experience, which was very upsetting for a New England clergyman.

Dr. Joy brought me word that Major Torr's plan for getting British soldiers out of Spain was no longer working. I was to send no more British soldiers across the frontier. Rather, from now on, I was to send them directly to Gibraltar by sea. I saw Fitch that same evening and told him the news, and he turned his attention to boats the next day. We put Dick Ball to work on the project, too. Dick's ability to speak the tough French slang of the port made him a good candidate for the job.

The following week Dick found a solution to our problem — a trawler, with an auxiliary motor, large enough to take seventy-five persons to Gibraltar. Dick had found it through a Frenchman he met in Snappy's Bar, a favorite hangout of the British officers in Marseilles. The Frenchman, who went by the name of the "Baron," professed to be an ardent anti-Nazi. He put Dick in touch with the captain and crew of the boat. It wasn't until Dick was convinced the whole thing was absolutely on the level that he came to me about it.

I didn't believe it at first. The whole thing seemed just a little too good to be true. Here was a large, seaworthy fishing boat with good, strong sails, a motor in working order, enough oil already on board to make the long trip, and the right to go out of the harbor at any time to fish.

Then I discovered that Colonel Randolfo Paciardi, the leader of the Italian republicans in exile, had faith in the boat. In fact he, too, had been negotiating with the "Baron" and was sure that the whole deal was honest. When I told Fitch about it, he looked the boat over and brought back the same enthusiastic report.

In the end, I agreed to take a chance on it, but only on one condition: No money should be paid over until all the passengers were on board, and the ship was clear of the harbor. Fitch and Ball readily agreed to this condition. I gave Fitch money from the $10,000 the Ambassador had given me to pay for the British soldiers, and from the Committee's funds I gave Ball enough to pay for our refugees. The total amounted to nearly $3,000 at the current black market rate.

We arranged to put sixty British soldiers and fifteen refugees on the ship. Included among the refugees were the Bernhards, who were still hiding out in the tourist hotel. Also included was Baby, who was still supposed to be sick and confined to his room at the Splendide. Each passenger was to bring food and water enough to last for four days. Everybody was to gather after dark in a boathouse in back of the lighthouse near the outer harbor. The ship was to come down the various basins to the harbor shortly after midnight and pick up the passengers.

Just in case something should go wrong, I went out of town again that weekend the boat sailed. If the police questioned me later, I wanted to be able to say not only had I had nothing to do with the boat, but that I had been on a casual holiday when the escape occurred. If I stayed in Marseilles, I would inevitably be the center of the conspiracy. There was no use inviting arrest, at least until my successor arrived from the States. Much as I wanted to stay and be on hand for the escape, I took the train to Tarascon on Sunday morning.

On the way back to Marseilles the next afternoon, I half expected to be met at the station by a delegation from Police Headquarters waiting to arrest me for the crime of helping British soldiers escape from France. But there was no police delegation there, nor was there anyone from the office waiting for me at the Splendide. Had they all been arrested? I couldn't telephone to find out, and I couldn't go down to the office dressed in my hiking clothes. It would look too much as though I knew that something special was afoot.

I was quickly changing my clothes when somebody tapped very gently on the door of my room. I opened it and found Baby outside, looking as though his last hour had come. I knew then that something had gone wrong.

Baby came in, sat down, and told me as calmly as he could what had happened.

They had all met in the boathouse after dark as scheduled. It was a terrible night, cold and with a high wind. They had waited there in the wind and the dark, the sixty British soldiers, the Bernhards, Baby himself, and the others, until two o'clock in the morning. Then Beamish had come and told them it was all off. They had all gone back to town, one or two at a time, to avoid attracting the attention of the police.

Beamish told me more of the story an hour later at the office. There had been long conferences in Snappy's Bar, with the captain claiming he couldn't get the boat from the owner until the money had been paid. Fitch refused to pay a single franc until everybody was safely on board. But Dick Ball, after talking again to the captain, had persuaded Fitch to turn his money over. Then Dick gave the captain the money I had given him for our refugees. The captain took all the money and went out saying he would give it to the owner and come back with the boat.

He never came back.

22
The Villa Air-Bel

The first time I saw the Villa Air-Bel it was closed as tight as a fortress. The walks and gardens were overrun with weeds, and the hedges hadn't been trimmed in years. But the view across the valley to the Mediterranean was enchanting. The terrace, with its enormous plane trees, had a double flight of steps that led down, right and left, to a formal garden and a fish pond.

Beamish was opposed to the whole idea of my moving in. It was half an hour from town, and there was no telephone. He thought I ought to be more easily available in case of emergency. Of course he was right, but I was fed up with being available day and night. I had to have a little rest, at least a few hours a day. Otherwise I risked becoming so nervous and depressed that I would no longer be able to go on working.

It would have been hard to find a better place to rest and relax than the Villa Air-Bel. It was Indian summer. The days were fair, the sky blue, and the sun was so warm that on Sundays we often had lunch out-of-doors. But there was not only the house, the view, and the garden; there was also the group of people we assembled.

There was Victor Serge, a keen-minded old Bolshevik. During his long career, he had evolved from an extreme revolutionary to a moderate democrat. He told of his various experiences in Russian prisons. He recalled conversations with Trotsky. He knew all about the European secret police, and would tell us many stories about them. Listening to him was like reading a Russian novel.

André Breton was the dean of surrealist painters. He had been a doctor in the French Army during World War I. At Air-Bel, he made collections of insects, pieces of broken china polished by the sea, and old magazines. On his first day in the villa, Breton caught a scorpion in the bathtub. On another day, he placed a bottle of live praying mantises on the dining room table, in place of flowers.

Danny Bénédite, his English-born wife, Theodora, and their charming three-year-old son, Pierre, moved in with us, too. Danny claimed to be an authority on three subjects: wine, women, and politics. And he had very decided opinions on each.

Danny's friend and army comrade, the blond and taciturn Jean Gemahling, gave most of his attention to the women who shared the house with us and blushed scarlet whenever anyone spoke to him at dinner.

Jacqueline Breton, André's surrealist wife, was blonde and beautiful and savage. She had brightly painted toenails, and wore necklaces of tiger's teeth and tiny bits of mirror glass in her hair. Aube, their five-year-old daughter, was already hailed by the surrealist painters as a promising artist.

Laurette Séjourén, Victor Serge's friend, was a woman as unlike Jacqueline as Jacqueline was unlike everybody else. She was dark and quiet and very reserved. Although she generally stayed in her room during meals, professing not to be interested in food, the servants reported a large consumption of leftovers between meals.

The household was completed by Mary Jayne Gold, the charmer who had gotten Paul Hagen's friends out of Vernet. Mary Jayne was obviously enjoying everything, and not least the danger we were all in. And then there was Miriam Davenport, who laughed and coughed and shrieked until at last she left for Yugoslavia to marry a young art student she had met in Paris before the war.

On Sunday afternoons, André Breton invited the surrealist painters to the villa. The entire Deux Magots crowd came, and they were mad as ever: Oscar Dominguez, a large Spaniard who was living in a nearby villa with his fat and elderly, but rich, French girlfriend; Benjamin Péret, the French poet whose verses sometimes read as though they had been copied down from the walls of public toilets; Wilfredo Lam, the tragic-masked Cuban Negro who was one of the very few pupils Picasso ever took;

Victor Brauner, the one-eyed Rumanian painter whose women and cats all have one eye; and many others.

André would get out his collection of old magazines, colored papers, pastel chalks, scissors, and pastepots, and everybody would make montages, draw, or cut out paper dolls. At the end of the evening, André would decide who had done the best work, crying *"Formidable!" "Sensationel!"* or *"Invraisemblable!"* at each drawing, montage, or cutout in turn, chuckling with merriment all the while.

Then we would sit around drinking wine and singing. Danny knew the words and music to all the old French songs, and we spent many hours singing them. One that I remember in particular was "Passant par Paris." I can never whistle this song, even today, without having before my eyes a vivid picture of the dingy dining room, and Danny and Jean leaning back in their chairs singing the beautiful refrain.

We all knew that Villa Air-Bel was a temporary home. Half of its inhabitants were waiting for visas so they could escape from France. But it served as a wonderful haven for all of us. We were away from the center of Marseilles where things were rapidly getting worse and worse. For a few hours each day it provided us with a refuge from all the signs of the horror that was to come.

23
The "F" Route

The visa situation improved somewhat after the first of November, when both Spain and Portugal eased up on their restrictions. However, now it was necessary to take extreme caution in crossing the French frontier. There everything had changed. The good old days of August and early September were gone forever. There were no longer any friendly officials at the railway station, and the border itself was patrolled by guards who were more likely to use their rifles than point out the path to Spain.

It was during this time that Beamish and I organized the "F" route. Johannes Fittko was a German Social Democrat who had smuggled underground workers in and out of Germany across the Dutch border before and during the war.

We contacted Fittko and requested that he and his wife go down to Banyuls on the French border. They were able to do this because they had beautiful

French identity cards, made for them by our little Austrian cartoonist, Bill Freier. The identity cards made Mr. and Mrs. Fittko French citizens from the forbidden zone, where no Frenchman could go to check up on their credentials.

Banyuls, a town on the frontier, is the center of the district where the sweet grapes for the wine of that name are grown. Fittko and his wife established themselves as French refugees who could not return to their homes. They became friendly with their neighbors, worked in the vineyards, and often took jobs in fields near the frontier. On weekends, they walked in the hills and studied all the trails, observing the habits of the frontier guards. Soon they knew every footpath well and at what hours the guards patrolled what area. When they had everything set, they gave us a prearranged signal, and we began sending refugees down to them.

We provided the refugees with Freier identity cards so that they would not risk arrest on the way. We also gave each of our departing refugees a torn slip of colored paper with a number on it. Fittko had the other half of this paper. The refugee gave his half to Fittko. If the papers fitted together and had the same number, Fittko knew that the person came from us and was not a police stooge or Gestapo agent trying to discover our system of escape over the "F" route.

Fittko had already told his neighbors in Banyuls that he would have many French friends visiting him. He explained that his friends were refugees from the forbidden zone and, like him, could not *rejoindre leurs foyers* — rejoin their hearths — as the official phrase had it. The neighbors were sympathetic and welcomed the refugees as they would have welcomed any French citizens driven from their homes by the Germans. They readily offered them work in their fields and vineyards.

Dressed as farm laborers, or country people on a holiday, Fittko and the refugees would go out in the early morning. The refugees carried their few possessions in colored handkerchiefs or string bags as though they were loaves of bread and bottles of wine for lunch. Sometimes they would work in the fields all day. At other times they would go straight to the hills for a picnic.

After dark, Fittko would come back to Banyuls alone. If anyone asked, he would explain that his friends had had to return unexpectedly to their temporary homes in other towns. Generally he wasn't even asked. He did his work so skillfully that no one was suspicious of him.

In the course of about six months, Fittko passed more than one hundred people over the frontier this way. Not a single one of them was arrested, or even questioned by the police.

24
Journey into the Night

What were we to do about our protégés who were in concentration camps? How could we get them released? We decided to use a campaign of pressure on the Vichy government. We sent Danny Bénédite on a trip around southwest France. He visited the concentration camps and wrote long reports on the conditions he found there. At the same time, in the office, we prepared a list of our most distinguished refugees who were interned in these camps.

Danny found the conditions in the French camps worse than even he believed they would be. There was no deliberate torture, as there was everything else. There was cold, hunger, and disease. Everywhere there were lice, fleas, and bedbugs. In some camps, the men slept on damp sand. The food was very small in quantity and terrible in quality. One man wrote that rat meat had become a much-sought-after delicacy in his camp. The sanitary conditions were so bad that all the prisoners suffered from dysentery, and typhoid was practically epidemic.

In these camps were many of our most distinguished people, men like Peter Pringsheim, one of Europe's leading physicists and the brother-in-law of Thomas Mann; Erich Itor-Kahn, the noted pianist; Paul Westheim, the art critic and historian; and Wolf Leslau, one of the very few scholars who knew Amharic, the official language of Ethiopia.

Armed with Danny's reports and our lists of prominent internees, Marcel Chaminade and I set out for Vichy in mid-November. We wanted to see if we couldn't shame the French government into releasing our people. Getting them released from the camps was all we could hope for. We knew the government would not give them permission to leave the country, since literally no one was leaving France legally. Of course, once we got them out of the camps, Beamish and I had other plans for them. But not even Chaminade knew that.

There was still another reason for my wanting to go to Vichy. I wanted to find out what my own position was. The American Consul had warned me not to travel without police permission. I applied for this permission, but it was not granted, so in the end I decided to go without it.

The Consul said, "You are putting your head in the lion's mouth."

But I wasn't as sure as he was that I'd be arrested when I got off the train at the Vichy station.

I still believed in the prestige of America.

Going to Vichy was like making a journey into the night. The town was filled with rumors, fear, and intrigue — as well as crowds of people. We trudged from hotel to hotel until we were ready to give up hope of finding rooms. Then we came into the Hotel Albert Premier just as somebody was unexpectedly checking out. We grabbed his room.

There was no heat in our room, and in the mornings there was never any hot water. It was about as cozy as a butcher's refrigerator.

We set about our work methodically. We tried to get a typewriter to copy Danny's reports on the concentration camps, but the only machine we could find had a keyboard printed in Hungarian. We finally sent for Lena to come up from the office with a typewriter. When she had typed up the reports, we left a copy with every official we called on.

At the Ministry of the Interior we were refused an audience with the Minister. Instead, we saw Dr. Limousin, a pasty-faced young fascist who was in charge of the concentration camps. When we told him about the camps, he bristled.

"What is wrong with our concentration camps?" he asked. "The Nazi authorities have congratulated us on them. May I ask what you find wrong with them?"

At the end of two weeks we had to admit that we had been given the runaround everywhere. It was impossible to get anyone out of a concentration camp legally unless he already had an exit visa, and the government was mysterious and obviously embarrassed about exit visas.

The Chargé d'Affairs at the American Embassy was always too busy to see me. Finally, I saw the Third Secretary.

"We can't do anything for you, Mr. Fry," he said. "You don't seem to realize that the police have a dossier on you."

I told him the police had a dossier on everybody. Then I asked him if he knew what was in mine. He answered that I was suspected of helping refugees escape from France.

"You must understand," he said, "that we maintain friendly relations with the French government. Naturally, under the circumstances, we can't support an American citizen who is helping people evade French law. We sympathize with the desire of these poor unfortunates to find a haven overseas, but there is nothing we can do."

As my own French visa had just expired, I asked about having it renewed while I was in Vichy. I was told to go back to Marseilles and make an application at Police Headquarters there.

Two weeks of hard work had accomplished nothing. We decided to go back to Marseilles.

The train back was so crowded that we had to stretch out on the floor of the corridor. We were separated from one another by the bodies of other sleeping passengers. All through the night we were chilled by the drafts and the total absence of heat.

In the morning, Lena reported that she had been

annoyed half the night by a Frenchman who wanted to make love to her right there in the corridor, and couldn't understand why she refused.

Somehow, after the atmosphere of Vichy, it was good to have this reminder that we were still in France.

25
The Marshal
Comes to Town

Marshal Pétain was due in town on a Tuesday.
It was announced that he would spend the day in
Marseilles and then go to Toulon to inspect the fleet.
He would return to Marseilles the next day on his
way back to Vichy.

When Beamish heard the news, he decided to
leave town. "I always make it a practice to clear
out when the head of a fascist state comes to town,"
he said. "I know from long experience what
happens."

On Monday, he went down to the frontier to look
over some new routes, in case the "F" route should
be discovered and closed. I stayed in Marseilles.

It was a crisp December day, and there was a
heavy mist in our valley. The roofs of the houses
and the tops of the umbrella pines emerged out of
the feathery whiteness in receding planes of lighter
and lighter gray, like the peaks of mountains in a

Japanese print. You couldn't see the cemetery or the sea at all.

I had arranged to work at Air-Bel that Monday morning. Lena had agreed to come out and take dictation. So after breakfast, when Danny and Jean left for the office, I went up to my room to work. By ten o'clock there was still no sign of Lena. I was just about to give her up and go down to the office myself when she arrived.

"*Mille pardons,*" she said. "But I have been arrested this morning. That is why I am *tellement en retard.*"

"Arrested?" I asked. "What do you mean?"

"*Oui,* arrested," she said. "There are enormous raids going on in town. They came to the hotel early this morning and made us all go downstairs in our nightgowns. They kept us there for hours while they looked over our papers. *Finalement* they let me go. But many they took away."

"What's the idea?" I asked.

"It is the visit of Marshal Pétain tomorrow," she said.

"Oh," I said. "Well, it's too bad for our refugees. We'll have to try and get them released this afternoon. Meanwhile, let's get to work."

I had finished the first letter and was beginning the second when someone tapped on the door.

Lena got up and opened the door. It was one of the maids.

"Excuse me, *monsieur,* but the police are downstairs," she said.

"*Mon dieu!* Have I got to go through that again?" Lena asked.

"Let's finish this letter before we go down," I said.

"At your service," Lena said, picking up her notebook and pencil again.

We were just finishing the letter when Victor Serge appeared in the door.

"The police insist that everyone in the house assemble in the grand hall at once," he said.

I gave a quick glance around the room. On the table was my address book. It had the names and addresses of almost everyone I'd met in France, as well as detailed records of all my illegal financial transactions. I knew that address books often interest the police more than anything else. It was with real pain that I threw it into the fire, and we stood there watching it flame up. When it was burned to ashes, we went downstairs together.

We found everybody else in the house already assembled in the entrance hall. Standing at the door, as though to bar our exit, was an enormous police official. Near him were three plainclothesmen. Everybody, including the police official and the plainclothesmen, looked very nervous.

"Well, is that all?" the official asked in a loud, bullying voice, addressing the housekeeper.

"Yes, sir, that's all," she answered in her soft, superior-servant tone.

"*Alors, procédez,*" the official shouted as though drunk.

"Proceed to what?" I asked.

"To search the house, of course," he yelled.

"May I ask," I said, "by what authority you expect to search this house?"

"We have the authority," he bellowed. "Don't you worry yourself about that."

"I should nevertheless like to see your papers."

"Oh, so you want to make trouble, do you?" he sneered.

"Not at all," I said, growing extremely excited, and speaking the French words with exaggerated precision and very slowly. "But I wish to insist upon my rights and the rights of my friends. We have nothing to hide. But we will not submit to a search unless you have written orders to conduct one."

He reached into his inner pocket and pulled out a soiled and folded paper. He handed it to me with a flourish.

"*Voilà, monsieur*," he said, with mocking courtesy.

I took the paper and unfolded it. Victor and Lena looked over my shoulder as I read it.

It was a carbon copy of an order to the chief of police authorizing him to search all premises "suspected of Communist activity."

"This order does not apply to us," I said. "These premises are not suspected of Communist activity. You have no right to search them. I refuse to permit you to do so."

"That's where you're wrong," he bawled back at me. "These premises *are* suspected of Communist activity, and I intend to search the house from top to bottom."

He turned to his men and barked "Proceed!"

One of the plainclothesmen sat at a small table in the center of the room and began to write out our names, using a separate paper for each individual or family group. While this was going on, another plainclothesman took Victor upstairs to search his room.

When they came back, the plainclothesman was carrying a portable typewriter and a pearl-handled revolver. He showed them to his boss.

"Ah! Here's something already," the official said with a satisfied grin. "Continue."

André Breton was the next victim. He was led off to his room on the top floor.

Suddenly I remembered that among the books on my dresser there was a false passport. Somehow I had to get up there, alone, and get rid of it.

I decided to try the old trick. The nearest toilet was at the end of the hall next to the door of my room. I asked to be allowed to use it. The police official hesitated. Then he told one of the plainclothesmen to go upstairs with me.

On the way up I sounded out my guard. "Your boss seems a little rough," I said. "I wish he'd take it easy."

"I know," the man said. "He's always like that. A natural bully."

We had come to the door of the toilet. I went inside and closed the door. He waited outside.

How was I to get to my room without him? It would take only a few seconds to get rid of the passport once I was there, but I had to be alone. I decided to make a try at it. When I came out of the toilet, I said, "I have to get a handkerchief. I'll be right back." I ducked into my room.

Miraculously, he stayed where he was. "All right," he called. "Take your time."

I took the passport and threw it up onto the top of the wardrobe. There wasn't time for anything else. Then I opened the bureau drawer and took out a clean handkerchief. I was blowing my nose with it when I came out of the room.

"All right now?" the man asked.

"Yes," I said. "Thanks."

When we got downstairs again, André and his plainclothesman were already there. There was a large service revolver on the table beside Victor's pearl-handled one.

The next to go was Mary Jayne. While she was upstairs, the housekeeper asked permission to go to the kitchen with the maid and make coffee for everybody. The police official was in the dining room with Victor and André, inspecting the china. The only person watching us was the detective at the center table.

I sat down next to Lena.

"Engage that guy in conversation," I whispered. "I want a chance to go through my pockets."

"Okay," she said. "But when you finish, I want a chance to go through my pocketbook."

"All right," I said. "I'll do what I can."

She got up and walked over to the table.

"That's a nice suit you're wearing," she said. "In these days it's so hard to find anything to wear. Do you mind telling me where you bought it?"

The plainclothesman was obviously flattered. He beamed. "You like it?" he asked.

"Oh, yes," she said. "It's beautiful. Such nice material. Such good taste."

I was emptying my pockets into the fire in the tile stove.

"I have my own tailor," the plainclothesman confessed.

"You must be rich," Lena said.

He blushed. He was very blond, and his face was now very red. "Oh, no," he said. "He's not really expensive at all."

"Won't you write out his name and address for me?" Lena asked.

She was doing fine. I was almost through emptying my pockets.

The plainclothesman began writing on a slip of paper.

I picked up a log and pushed it into the stove after the last of my papers.

"*Voilà, mademoiselle,*" he said, handing Lena the address.

"Oh, thank you," Lena said. "You are so kind."

"It's nothing, *mademoiselle*, nothing at all," he said, smiling from ear to ear.

Lena came back to her chair next to mine. "Did you have enough time?" she whispered.

"Yes," I said. "Thanks a million. You did fine."

"*Maintenant*, it's your turn," she said.

I went up to the plainclothesman. "How long do you think this will last?" I asked.

"I don't know," he said.

"What's your boss going to do?"

"I think he's going to take you all down to headquarters."

"What for?"

"For control of your situations."

Out of the corner of my eye I could see Lena bending down to poke the fire. "What does that mean?" I asked.

"Just an inquiry. An examination of your papers. Then if all is in order, you will be released."

"I hope so," I said. "I haven't got much time to waste. How will we get down to headquarters?"

He got up from his chair and led me toward the window. "Look," he said.

I looked. Parked in front of the house were a large police van and a smaller police car. Standing between them was a fifth detective.

"All that for us?" I asked.

"Yes," he said, "all that for you."

"We must be pretty important," I said.

Behind me, I could hear the door of the stove close.

"What is it?" Lena asked, coming up behind us.

"We're just looking at the view," I said. "Have a look."

"*Mon dieu!*" she said. "I hadn't seen those before. Are they for us?"

"Yes," I said. "They're for us."

Just then the official came back from the dining room. "What's going on here?" he yelled.

The plainclothesman hurried back to his place at the table.

"Nothing," he said nervously.

When it came my turn to go upstairs, the official himself went up with me. He did not look on top of the wardrobe, but he gathered up all the papers on my table, and stuffed them into my briefcase. Then he carried the briefcase triumphantly downstairs, along with my portable typewriter.

"Documents in foreign languages," he said to the plainclothesman who was acting as the recording secretary of the expedition. "Probably revolutionary propaganda. Enter them!"

The plainclothesman entered them. Just then there was a stir outside. The official rushed out, followed by two of the plainclothesmen. Through the open door we could hear him shouting.

"Arrest them, I tell you, arrest them!"

A moment later the policeman came in again, leading Danny and Jean by the arms. They had come back to the house for lunch and had walked into the trap.

The official gathered up the typewriters, revolvers, and documents. "I am taking you all down to headquarters," he said.

We all protested loudly.

"It will only be for a short time," he said, suddenly changing his attitude. "You will all be back before nightfall. It's a mere formality." To me he adopted a tone which was almost pleading. "There is absolutely nothing against you," he said. "No suspicion of any sort. But you would oblige me by accompanying the others. Merely as witness. You will be able to return to your work within the hour. I give you my word of honor that I will not detain you longer."

Won over by his sudden politeness, and thinking I might be able to help the others if I went with them, I agreed to go. Had I had any idea of what was to happen, or how long it would be before we returned to the Villa Air-Bel, I would not have been nearly so agreeable.

26
Prisoners on
the S.S. *Sinaïa*

We all piled into the police van and were driven down to headquarters. There we were taken through the motorcycle garage and up a flight of stairs to a low-ceilinged room on the second floor. Many other prisoners were in the room, and from time to time more were led in. Toward the end of the afternoon, we were called one by one into a small office. We were asked to sign a list of what had been found in our rooms. Then we were taken back to the low-ceilinged room.

At six o'clock, a newspaper vendor came in. We persuaded him to go down to a nearby *bistro* and buy us wine and sandwiches. It was the first time we had had anything to eat or drink since the housekeeper's coffee.

By seven o'clock, we had begun to grow restless. We asked the guard if we could see the official and find out when he expected to release us. But the guard said the official had gone for the day.

"He won't be back until tomorrow morning," he said.

By eight o'clock, still nothing had happened. We were all angry and saying, "What are they doing to us?" And, "This is impossible." And worse!

At nine o'clock, we were all led downstairs again and around a corner to a small rear court. Then back into the building and upstairs to a large room. It was stuffed full of human beings, among them some of our refugees. It was obvious that an enormous raid was going on.

At eleven o'clock, we were taken downstairs again and back to the small rear court. There we were loaded into an even larger van than the one which had come for us at the house.

I sat next to one of the detectives. "Where are they taking us now?" I asked.

"I think they're taking you to a boat in the harbor," he said.

I now began to feel the sense of high indignation that Americans sometimes feel when they are not treated as superior beings in foreign lands. "This is an outrage," I said. "I am an American citizen. I demand to be allowed to communicate with my Consul."

"I'm afraid there isn't a thing I can do about that," the detective said.

"What can I do, then?" I asked weakly.

"Nothing, I'm afraid," he said.

After what seemed like an endless drive, we turned onto one of the docks. We drew up alongside a ship, black and forbidding in the semidarkness.

Here we were ordered out of the van and led up the ship's ladder to the main deck. Once we were on board, the detectives returned to the dock and drove off in the van.

We found ourselves in a dense and milling crowd of puzzled humanity. We learned that we were on the S.S. *Sinaïa*, along with some six hundred other prisoners. All of them were as baffled as we were. No one knew why we had been arrested or where we were to be taken. All we knew was that for women there were third-class cabins, and for the men, bunks in the hold.

As there seemed no point in standing on the deck all night, we went to bed. We slept in our clothes, on burlap bags filled with straw. Each of us had a single thin blanket for his only cover. The hatch was uncovered, and we could look up through the square opening at the stars above our heads. In one corner of the hold, a group of Spaniards were singing sad flamencos to the music of an out-of-tune guitar. It was very cold, and the dirt in the straw got under our clothes and made us itch.

In the morning, we were told that in order to get food we had to form into groups of ten and elect a leader who would go to the galley for the whole group. We elected André, and he went off in the direction of the galley. Half an hour later he came back carrying a loaf of black bread and a large tin pail half full of a light-brown liquid sweetened with saccharine. For lunch we were given frozen beef, lentils, bread, and wine. For dinner, in addition to the beef, there was also soup. The beef, though hot on the outside, was still frozen in the center.

We spent the day trying to persuade someone in authority to let us call the American Consulate. But the only person in authority we could find was the guard at the head of the ladder. He told us he had strict orders not to allow anyone on board to communicate with anyone on shore under any circumstances.

In the afternoon of the second day, we were all ordered below. When we got there, they put the cover over the hatch and closed all the portholes. We thought we were about to set sail for Africa and a concentration camp in the Sahara — but the boat didn't move. Then we heard many whistles blowing in the harbor.

After several hours we were allowed to go up on deck again. There we learned from a member of the crew that Marshal Pétain had gone by in a coast-guard cutter while we were below.

Toward evening, some boys from the town came to the ship's side to take orders for food. We wrote out a message to the American Consul. Then we wrapped it around a ten-franc piece. We threw it overboard while the guard at the head of the ladder had his back turned. We decided the chances were ten to one that the boy who picked it up would pocket the coin and throw the message away, but a few hours later a large package of sandwiches arrived for us. Inside the package was the calling card of the American Consul-General. We were grateful for the sandwiches, though we would have preferred freedom.

On the third day we still had no news of what was to become of us. We spent the day speculating on our fate and singing old French songs to while away the time. By afternoon, Mary Jayne and I managed to send a note up to the captain. We got back an invitation to call on him in his cabin. It was a strange sensation to sit in chairs, after so many hours on wooden benches, the edges of iron bunks, and the rail of a ship.

The captain was most apologetic to his American prisoners. He was really upset when I told him I had once crossed the Atlantic on his ship.

"I am sorry you should have had to see it again under such very different circumstances," he said.

He explained that the Administration had hired his ship as a prison. He was in no way responsible for the choice of passengers, nor had he any idea how long we would be held.

"This is out of my power to determine," he said.

As we were talking, a cabin boy came in and announced that *Monsieur le Consul des Etats-Unis* was waiting below.

The captain was very much impressed. He told the boy to bring the American Consul up at once.

When Harry Bingham, the Consul, walked through the door and shook hands with us, whatever doubts the captain may have had about us were immediately dispelled. He became much more cordial. He took out a key and unlocked a cupboard which held a large collection of half-filled bottles. He selected a bottle of cognac and took down four small glasses. As we drank, Harry told us he had called the head of the police several times to find out why we were being held, but all the high officials were with the Marshal, or busy protecting him. So Harry hadn't been able to get any information. However, tomorrow the Marshal would be on his way back to Vichy and things would be returning to normal in Marseilles. A great many people had been arrested in honor of the Marshal's visit, he said, at least seven thousand. Most of them would probably be released in a few days. Whether we would be released or not he couldn't say, but he would do his best to see that we were.

We went to bed that night still not knowing whether it would be our last night on the *Sinaïa* or not. But about ten o'clock the next morning, some detectives arrived with fat dossiers under their arms. They took over the first-class lounge and began calling individuals by name from the eager crowd waiting on the third-class deck below.

Our group was called about noon, and by two o'clock in the afternoon we had all been released. We walked down the long pier toward the trolley-car line. When we got to the center of town, we found the streets still decorated with flags, and the street cleaners at work cleaning up the litter left behind by the crowds. Members of the Garde Pétain were still swaggering around, wearing white brassards on their arms with the letters G.P. on them.

After lunch, Jean Gemahling and I dropped into the office, and the others returned to the villa. We found everything perfectly normal at the office. Contrary to our worst fears, it had not been closed.

In fact, the police had never even gone near it. None of the members of the staff, except those who lived in Air-Bel, had been arrested, yet hardly a refugee had shown his face at the office after word got around that we had been taken away.

Elsewhere there had been police action amounting literally to hysteria. Three more boats, four forts, and three movie houses, in addition to all the regular jails and prisons, had been filled with people arrested. At the last minute, before the Marshal appeared, the police had even locked people into cafés and restaurants until he had passed.

In all, twenty thousand people had been arrested. The Marshal's visit had been a huge success.

27
The Kidnapping
at Cannes

For two weeks after the *Sinaïa* affair I was followed by a group of eight plainclothesmen, working
in shifts. Captain Dubois told me about it. He said
the order had come directly from the National Police
at Vichy. Thanks to Dubois's tip-off, I saw to it that
the *flics'* daily reports were pretty dull. They told
mostly where I had lunch and where I had dinner
every day.

After a couple of weeks, the police got tired of
this and called the whole thing off. But while it
lasted it was uncomfortable, and I had to be very
careful of what I did and whom I saw.

As soon as I learned I was being followed, I
warned everybody to be extremely wary. Mary
Jayne was so nervous she kept looking back over
her shoulder all the rest of the day. As a result,
three Frenchmen, who were not detectives at all,
followed her for considerable distances.

One day toward the middle of the month, two

plainclothesmen came into my office, showing their badges. I asked them what they wanted. They said they were looking for a man named Hermant. Fortunately, Beamish was still out of town. I asked them why they were interested in him. They said there were some serious charges against him. Then they added, "If you see him again, let us know."

I solemnly promised I would.

When Beamish got back to Marseilles, I told him the story, and he decided the time had come for him to say good-bye to France. We took a sad leave of one another, and he set off for the "F" route at Banyuls. A few days later I learned that he had reached Lisbon safely.

I felt peculiarly lonely after Beamish left. I suddenly realized how completely I had come to rely on him. Not only did I count on him to help with the most difficult problems, but I also depended on him for companionship. He was the only person in France who knew exactly what I was doing, and why, and for this reason he was the only one with whom I could always be at ease. With everyone else I had to pretend — sometimes more, sometimes less. With Beamish, and Beamish only, I could be perfectly free and natural. Now he was gone. I was completely alone. I felt my solitude as I had never felt it before.

In mid-December, Pierre Laval, Head of the French Cabinet at Vichy, was arrested. Marshal Pétain ordered him seized by the police at the end of a Cabinet meeting and taken to his house where he was held under guard.

The morning the news broke, there were excited groups on all the street corners of Marseilles. Rumors of every kind flew fast, and most of them proved false. But the rumor that Marseilles would be occupied by the Germans on the first of January persisted. We sensed lightning in the air. We knew that, whatever happened, things were not likely to get better for the refugees and the French who had refused to accept the policy of collaboration.

All in all, we still felt it was a good idea for people to get out of France if they could, by any method available. Not everybody agreed with us, however. Among the most stubborn stayers-on were some of the most important people on our lists.

André Gide was one of these men. He was living in a town high in the mountains back of Cannes. We went to see him. He was greatly depressed by the fate that had befallen France, and he told us that the Germans had been making determined efforts to get him to collaborate. They were using flattery and soft gloves instead of threats and the mailed fist. But Gide said he had refused and always would refuse to collaborate. Because the Germans realized Gide's position as dean of French letters, they wanted to win him over, but Gide was determined to reject all the Nazis' advances to him. He knew the possible consequences of his decision. He nevertheless refused to leave France. It was his home, and he was determined to stay.

Although he thanked us for all we were doing for other writers, he flatly refused to let us persuade him to become one of our "clients." The best we could do was get him to agree to let us know immediately if he had any serious trouble with the authorities, French or German.

At Nice, on our return trip to Marseilles, we were greeted with the news that something had happened to Fritz Thyssen, the German industrialist who had long backed Hitler, but who had turned against Hitler and the whole Nazi party when the war broke out. The newspaper announced that the Ministry of the Interior at Vichy had denied that Mr. and Mrs. Thyssen had been arrested.

"If Mr. and Mrs. Thyssen have been obliged to report to the local police station," the newspaper quoted the Ministry as saying, "it can only have been for the periodic control required of all foreigners."

"If I know anything about fascist journalism," Valeriu Maru, the Rumanian historian who was with me, said, "that means the Thyssens have been arrested. Why don't you stop off at Cannes and find out?"

By the time I got to Cannes, night had already fallen. I went to the Thyssens' hotel and asked at the desk for Mr. Thyssen.

"Mr. Thyssen has left. Are you a friend of his, sir?" the clerk said.

I said I was an American journalist who wanted to interview him.

"Then you haven't heard the news?" the man asked, raising his eyebrows.

"What news?" I asked, playing innocent.

"I'm afraid I can't tell you," the clerk said. "You'd better talk to the boss."

As soon as he had telephoned upstairs for the boss, I moved toward the entrance door.

"I'll wait outside," I said.

Outside, the doorman was more communicative. He said that on Friday morning at seven o'clock five plainclothesmen had come to the hotel in two automobiles bearing Vichy license plates. As soon as the Thyssens came downstairs, the plainclothesmen placed them under arrest, ordered them to pack a few clothes, and then drove off with them in the direction of Vichy.

"Where do you think they were taking them?" I asked.

"To the Boches," he said.

Just then the clerk called me inside. The "boss" was short and fat and very conventional looking. He pleasantly asked me what he could do for me. When I told him I had come to find out about the Thyssens, his whole manner changed abruptly. "I regret," he said coldly, "that I can give you no information. I have given my word of honor not to speak of it to anyone."

"To whom did you give that word?" I asked.

"To the agents who arrested them," he said.

"The local agents?"

"No. Agents from Vichy," he said.

"Oh," I said. "They came all the way down from Vichy to get them?"

"I can say nothing. Absolutely nothing," the man said. He was irritated at having been trapped into admitting this much.

"But this is important," I said. "Don't you realize that lives may be at stake?"

"I realize only that I have given my word of honor not to talk. And I intend to keep it."

"There is a higher honor than your word to the police," I said. "The honor of France."

"Come, come," he said officiously. "You are an agreeable young man. Come to my bar and have as many drinks as you like at my expense. Be my guest at dinner. But, please, don't ask me any questions about Mr. and Mrs. Thyssen. I can't answer them."

"I have not come for free drinks," I said. "I have come to find out what became of the Thyssens."

"That," he said, growing visibly excited, "you will never learn from me. Now get out! Get out of my hotel, I tell you, before I have you thrown out!"

He was advancing toward me menacingly.

"By refusing to talk you are doing the work of the Nazis," I said.

"Don't you dare come here and tell me what to do and what not to do," he shouted. "Why don't you go back where you came from, anyway, and leave us French alone? If we want to collaborate with the Germans, we will collaborate with the Germans, and nothing you pigs of Americans say will influence us in the slightest. Now get out, I tell you! Get out!"

I got out.

When I got back to Marseilles, I found the city

under a blanket of wet snow. In spite of the cold and the damp, an old woman was selling pamphlets on the corner of the boulevard.

"*Lisez 'la fin du monde,*' " she kept crying. "Read 'The End of the World.' "

28
A New Escape Route

For us and our work it really looked like the end of the world. The Thyssens were our first verified case of an extradition — a surrender on demand — by the French police. There had been no warning to the victims, in fact, every precaution had been taken to catch them unawares. It was virtually an official kidnapping. Now the bars were down. How many others would soon follow the Thyssens on the long road north?

I passed a restless night wondering where the Gestapo would strike next. How could we possibly get the rest of our people out before they, too, were caught and carried off to Germany? I had nightmares all night. I woke up again and again with my heart pounding in my chest and the sound of a knock at the door ringing in my ears. But when I went to the door, still trembling with the fear of the dream, there was no one there.

I spent Christmas and the days immediately following trying to find ways of getting large numbers of refugees out of France without waiting any longer for American or other overseas visas. Captain Fitch had left France, and Captain Murphy was now in charge of evacuating the remaining British soldiers in Marseilles. He wanted to find ways to send his men to Africa and the Near East, rather than through Spain. He figured from Africa his men could somehow make their way to Gibraltar by sea or to Palestine or Egypt overland.

Jean Gemahling and I used to meet Captain Murphy late at night in a back room at the Dorade. Charles, the owner, would join us. Charles's smuggling had made him thoroughly familiar with the port and its ways. He knew most of the dock workers and at least some of the members of the crew of every ship. He said it would be an easy matter for him to smuggle refugees and British soldiers onto ships bound for Beirut, Algiers, Oran, and Casablanca. For each passenger he wanted from 3,000 to 8,000 francs, depending on the length of the voyage and the risks involved.

We used the British for guinea pigs first because they ran smaller risks than the refugees. At worst, they would only be interned for the duration of the war. The refugees would be tortured and killed, and no one would have the right even to complain.

We sent the British all over the Mediterranean: to Syria, North Africa, Gibraltar, Rabat, and Casablanca, even to Dakar. Those who got to Gibraltar jumped off the French ships as they passed the Rock and swam ashore. But most of them went on to the

French ports, and most of them were arrested there. At least they were released when the American troops invaded North and West Africa. If they had stayed in Marseilles, they would have been taken to Germany.

From the experience gained with the British, it was evident that Charles could perform what he promised. There was never a slip in Marseilles, and never, as far as I know, a slip at the other end either — so far as getting off the ships was concerned.

What we lacked was organization in the ports of destination. When the British were arrested, it was because they had nowhere to go when they left the ships. Although Charles always provided them with crew cards and clothes, he could not provide them with hiding places in cities other than Marseilles.

For the British this was unfortunate, but it did not matter so much with the refugees. We could give them false identity cards, and, since most of them could speak French, they ran little risk of being arrested once they arrived. To give the British false identity cards would have been to court double disaster — for them and for us. Not one of them could possibly be mistaken for a Frenchman by anybody.

29
The Ship
to Martinique

One of our principal difficulties was that we had
no way of knowing who was really in immediate
danger. Georg Bernhard was the only person in
France whom we definitely knew was wanted by
the Gestapo. I urged him to go to Africa, but he
refused to leave without his wife. I asked Charles
if he could smuggle a woman on board one of the
cargo ships. He said there was no way to do this.
Besides, he wanted nothing to do with women; they
always caused trouble. So the Bernhards had to
wait until I could find some other way to get them
out of France.

However, the arrest and extradition of Mr. and
Mrs. Thyssen gave us a basis for evaluating relative
danger. Berlin and Madrid, it seemed, were determined to get their hands on the top leaders of their
exiled nationals first. The problem, then, was to see
who were the next most prominent Germans after
the Thyssens. The answer was the two Rudolfs:

Breitscheid and Hilferding. Both of them were still living in forced residence at the Hotel Forum in Arles.

Saving Breitscheid and Hilferding was bound to be extremely difficult, even if they were now willing to be saved. Both of them were so well known they risked being recognized by the average German, Gestapo agent or otherwise. Yet, if we could get them to Marseilles, we could disguise them with makeup and hair dye and put them on one of the cargo ships to Africa.

The real problem was to get them out of Arles, onto a ship, and away before they were missed and the alarm was spread. Obviously they couldn't travel on a train. The only automobiles that were moving belonged either to the French police or to members of the German and Italian armistice commissions. No taxi was allowed outside the city limits.

I took the problem to Charles, who said it was easy. One of his gangster friends had a big limousine licensed for driving throughout the neighboring country any time of the day or night, seven days a week. This was an unheard of privilege. Even the busiest collaborating Marseilles manufacturer could drive his car only on alternate weekdays, and then only during the daylight hours. But Charles showed me the card of permission, and what he said proved to be perfectly true.

When everything was ready, we sent word of our plans to Arles. To our great relief, the two Rudolfs were willing to take the risks of going by cargo ship to North Africa. False identity cards were made for them so they could register safely at hotels in Algeria. Then we arranged a place and time for the gangster's car to pick them up on the night a cargo ship was sailing.

I had dinner at the Dorade that night and sat late at my table afterward waiting for news. By eleven o'clock, nothing had happened. Then the driver of the gangster's car appeared in the doorway. He was obviously furious. I watched him go over to Charles, who was sitting behind the cash register. Charles looked up from his account books. Because of the other people in the restaurant, I pretended to be showing no interest in their conversation.

"*Allez!* What's up?" I heard Charles say.

"They've changed their minds," I could hear the driver answer.

"What?" Charles asked, incredulous.

"They don't want to leave," the driver said.

"What do you mean, they don't want to leave?"

The driver shrugged. "That's what they said," he replied. "Here I go all the way out to Arles to get two men who are supposed to be in danger of their lives, and when I get there they tell me they've changed their minds! *Je me fous de ces gars-là. Ce sont des couillons!*" I'm so angry at those guys. They're jerks!

Charles said nothing at all. He just stirred himself a bicarbonate of soda.

We didn't have to wait long for an explanation. It came by mail the next day. Breitscheid and Hilferding had been making efforts through friends in the United States to obtain exit visas from France. In his letter from Arles, Hilferding wrote that he had just received a cable from America saying that the exit visas had been granted.

I was extremely skeptical about this piece of news and strongly inclined to doubt it. I had sent nearly 350 human beings out of France by this time, most of them without any exit visas at all and not one with an exit visa that would stand up under careful inspection. I had come to think of illegal emigration as the normal, if not the only, way to go.

But I was just an ordinary American with only as much authority as my moderate success at arranging escapes had given me. Breitscheid and Hilferding thought of themselves as great statesmen. They were not accustomed to taking orders from anybody. They were not even very favorably disposed to accepting polite suggestions — at least not when they came from me. The two men now dropped all thought of leaving France illegally and devoted all their attention to obtaining legal permission to go.

As soon as Hilferding received the cable from America, Breitscheid went to the head of the police at Arles. He asked if it would be safe to make formal application for exit visas and whether the applications would be submitted to the German authorities. The police head said he couldn't answer the question himself but would check with Vichy.

Two days later he told Breitscheid there would

be no danger at all; in fact, it was no longer necessary to even apply for exit visas. He had just received a telegram from Vichy saying the visas had been authorized. All Breitscheid and Hilferding had to do was go to Police Headquarters at Marseilles and pick them up.

When Breitscheid and Hilferding came into my office and showed me the exit visas the police had stamped on their American "affidavits in lieu of passport," I was properly embarrassed at my pigheaded insistence on extralegal and illegal methods. I was dismayed to think of the unnecessary and even foolish risks I had been persuading them to take. Hilferding was beaming, and the wax mask of Breitscheid's face came alive for the first time since I'd known him. Mrs. Breitscheid and Breitscheid's secretary, Erika Bierman, seemed even more pleased than the men.

Their exit visas specified that they should go by way of Martinique. The police chief had even given them a letter of introduction to a steamship company that was supposed to have a ship sailing for Fort de France on February 4.

Breitscheid and Mrs. Bierman went down to the office of the steamship company to make reservations. They were told that the only places left were bunks in a dormitory in the hold. As Breitscheid suffered from insomnia, and his wife wasn't well, he decided to wait for a later sailing. He left without making any reservations at all.

The next day we tried to persuade him to take any accommodations he could get, even if it meant unpleasantness and discomfort. But he refused to consider it. For the first time since I'd known him, Hilferding did not submit to Breitscheid's authority, but decided for himself. He went down to the steamship office and made a reservation in the dormitory. While he was there, he also tried to get places for the others in the hope that Breitscheid would change his mind before the boat sailed. The clerk said he would see what he could do, and would let him know the next day.

By now it was Tuesday evening. Breitscheid and Hilferding had had their passes to Marseilles prolonged a day. But they found they could get them extended no longer. They had to return to Arles that night or break the law. When I saw them for the last time, just before they left for Arles, Breitscheid was still determined not to sail if he had to bunk in the dormitory, and Hilferding was equally decided to take anything he could get.

On Wednesday, the clerk at the steamship company said he had been able to find a place for Hilferding in the dormitory, but could do nothing for Mr. and Mrs. Breitscheid and Mrs. Bierman, as it was now too late.

Early Friday morning there were four letters from Arles. The first one contained Hilferding's final plans for the trip. He said he would come to Marseilles on the morning of Saturday, February 1. Breitscheid's first letter also contained instructions and seemed to indicate he had changed his mind — too late — and had decided to go with Hilferding after all. The other two letters were very brief.

Both explained that on the afternoon of Thursday, January 30, the police at Arles had informed the two men that Vichy had ordered them to cancel their exit visas.

The ship for Martinique sailed on Tuesday, but none of our people from Arles sailed on it. It was little Walter Mehring who got the bunk in the hold that had been reserved for Hilferding.

A month later Baby was in New York.

30
Delivery to Death

What happened next in Arles has been told by Mrs. Breitscheid in a memorandum she wrote at my request less than two weeks after the event. Part of it reads:

"On Saturday evening, shortly before eleven o'clock, there was a loud knocking on our door. It was an official from the local police. He was very excited. He told us immediately to pack a couple of bags, as my husband must get away at once. The Gestapo was looking for him. The same thing happened to Hilferding. The man said I was not, under any circumstances, to be allowed to go with them. It was a strict order. . . .

"At the police station the chief of police said he knew nothing beyond the fact that an automobile was coming from Marseilles to take us away. . . .

"We finally set out and, in spite of the protests of the officials, I went along. We arrived at Vichy.

On the way my husband complained, 'Why do you torture us this way if you only want to extradite us in the end?'

"In Vichy we were taken to a hotel. There was no sign to identify it, but there is no doubt that it was a police hotel. I now had to separate from the two men. I was told I could inquire about my husband at two o'clock. But it was not until seven o'clock that I was able to talk to my husband. He told me they were to be extradited to Germany. . . .

"I was able to be with him a quarter of an hour, always in the presence of officials. Neither Hilferding nor my husband had any kind of hearing. There were no formal proceedings of any sort. But the police had taken away their razors, their medicines, and a letter opener. . . .

"After collecting myself a little, I ran to the American Embassy. It was Sunday evening, and there were only two porters there. I left a note to be given to the Ambassador as soon as possible. . . .

"From five until seven o'clock the following morning I walked up and down in front of the hotel that housed my husband. I did not want to miss him. . . .

"At seven o'clock, when the door was unlocked, I went in. I was able to speak with my husband and Hilferding until eight o'clock. I went to the American Embassy again, though naturally it was much too early. I added to the note what I begged them to do: intervene with Marshal Pétain's Cabinet, and also the police, to try and have the extraditions postponed; cable to Washington to bring pressure on the French. I begged the Ambassador or the Chargé d'Affaires to receive me and promised to return. . . .

"Then to the Ministry of the Interior. There the public was not permitted to ask for interviews until half past nine. Back to the American Embassy where the porter explained that the Secretary of the Embassy had asked him to tell me that there was unfortunately nothing to be done. Under the armistice the Germans had the right to demand the extraditions, and the French could only yield to this demand.

"Back to the Ministry of the Interior. I wrote out a slip of paper asking to be received. Reason: extradition of my husband. The usher refused to take my request to the Minister. It was forbidden.

"Hurried back to the hotel. It was a quarter to eleven. At eleven o'clock Hilferding and my husband were taken away. I left them a couple of minutes before, because my husband insisted on it. Again I could speak to both of them only in the presence of officials. They had taken Hilferding's poison away from him. But they had not found my husband's. He planned to take it only in the last extremity, but I am afraid the Germans will find it. From my hotel I watched the two autos drive away. . . ."

It had all happened so fast I knew nothing about it until I got to the office Monday morning. By that time it was already too late to do anything. Months later, I received a postcard from a friend telling me of Hilferding's death. His body, suspended from a hook in the ceiling by his necktie or belt, was found in a cell of the Santé Prison at Paris the day after Vichy handed him over to the Germans. Was it suicide? Or was it murder? I suppose nobody will ever know.

Three and a half years after the extraditions, the Germans announced that Breitscheid had been killed by American bombs during a raid on the concentration camp of Buchenwald.

How true was this announcement?

It is generally believed that Breitscheid, like Hilferding, was murdered on orders from Hitler.

31
Spring in Provence

Spring came early to Provence. Imperceptibly, the days lengthened, and the sun grew warmer. People began coming out of their damp unheated houses to greet the sun and the returning warmth. They began to write on the walls. V's, painted in bright red or indelible black, appeared on the walls of houses and the fronts of movie theaters and public buildings. And when one night the B.B.C. called on the French to write H's after the V's, for *"Vive l'honneur"* — Long Live Honor — VH's appeared all over Marseilles. It was called "the battle of the walls," and it went on for months and years, always taking new forms, never ceasing.

With spring there was also a new attitude toward the Germans. Instead of referring to them respectfully as the "occupying authorities," people began calling them *les doryphores* — the potato bugs — because they wore green and ate so greedily, and *les aspirateurs* — the vacuum cleaners — because they cleaned up everything in their path.

At Villa Air-Bel we had had to cut our food rations again and again, and like everybody else we began to develop signs of malnutrition. I lost twenty pounds and was hungry all the time.

Yet, with all its privations, life at the villa was immensely pleasant that spring. Before long, we were supplementing our poor meals with string beans, tomatoes, radishes, and lettuce fresh from our garden around the fish pool.

When some of those who lived in the house left France, others took their places. White-haired Max Ernst came down from St. Martin d'Ardèche, wearing a white sheepskin coat and bringing a great roll of his pictures which he tacked up in the drawing room. So we had a show that people came all the way from Marseilles to see.

Antoine de St. Exupéry's wife, Consuelo, arrived from nowhere one night and stayed for several weeks. She would climb trees and laugh and talk and scatter her money liberally among the poor artists.

Kay Boyle visited us on her periodic trips from Mégève in the French Alps to help an Austrian friend get his visas, and also to prepare for her own. She was like her novels: intense, emotional, and very finely wrought.

Peggy Guggenheim closed her museum of modern art at Grenoble and took Mary Jayne's room when Mary Jayne left for Lisbon and New York. Her conversation was a series of rapid, nervous questions.

Charles Wolff, a former feature writer for the *Luminère*, installed himself in a room on the top floor and consoled himself with many bottles of wine. He had had to leave a large collection of phonograph records in Paris when the Germans came. Whenever he thought of the Boches listening to his records, which was often, he took another drink.

At the end of May, we found that in less than eight months over 15,000 people had come to us or written to us. We had had to consider every one of their cases and make a decision on it. We had decided that 1,800 of the cases fell within the scope of our activities. In other words, these 1,800 were genuine cases of intellectual or political refugees with a good chance of emigrating soon. Of these 1,800 cases, representing in all some 4,000 human beings, we had paid weekly living allowances to 560 and sent more than 1,000 out of France. For the rest we had made every kind of effort, from getting them liberated from concentration camps to finding them a dentist.

We had more successes than failures that spring. Still I shall always think of it as a time of growing difficulties culminating in a series of crises and disasters.

32
The End of Dimitru

At the end of December, we had moved our office to larger quarters on the Boulevard Garibaldi. We became much more respectable and though the police might continue to suspect us, they could no longer call the office a "shady place."

Then, at the end of January, for some unexplained reason, many of the refugees discovered they could get exit visas. This meant the Gestapo had completed the task of going over the lists of refugees in France. They now knew which refugees they wanted and which they would allow to slip through their net.

Despite the new policy on exit visas, the attitude of the police toward the refugees became increasingly menacing as time passed. Early in April, they arrested all the Jews who were staying at Marseilles hotels and took them to the police station for "control of situation."

Fortunately, we had already gotten Georg Bernhard and his wife out of France and through Spain before this time.

Among those arrested, however, was Marc Chagall. He and his wife had come down from Gordes a few days before to get ready to leave France. They took a room at the Hotel Moderne. Early one morning the police arrived and arrested everybody in the hotel who seemed likely to be Jewish. They took Chagall away in the paddy wagon.

Mrs. Chagall called me about it almost as soon as I got to the office. I immediately telephoned an official at the station.

"You have just arrested Monsieur Marc Chagall," I said.

"So?"

"Do you know who Monsieur Chagall is?"

"No."

"He is one of the world's greatest living artists."

"Oh."

"If by any chance the news of his arrest should leak out," I went on, tingling with suppressed excitement at what I was saying, "the whole world would be shocked. Vichy would be gravely embarrassed, and you would probably be severely reprimanded."

"Thank you very much for calling me. I shall look into the case at once," the police official said.

Half an hour later the telephone rang. It was Mrs. Chagall. She said her husband had just returned to the hotel. Some time later, we got the Chagalls out of Marseilles and to the United States.

Others were not so lucky. They were placed in

forced residence or sent to concentration camps or forced-labor battalions.

When the British and the Free French launched their attack on Syria, the police began rounding up Frenchmen suspected of pro-British and pro-de Gaulle sympathies and putting them in concentration camps. A few days later it was announced that every person in France with two or more Jewish grandparents, whether French or foreigner, would have to fill out a long questionnaire listing, among other things, his bank accounts, securities, and real estate.

When Germany attacked Russia, all Russian émigrés were arrested, the Whites along with the Reds.

Early in May I was warned that the Jeunesse de France et d'Outre Mer, Vichy's fascist youth organization, was planning to raid our offices and smash them up — because we helped "Jews and dirty de Gaullists." I had Danny change the locks and put new and heavier bolts on all the doors. To make doubly sure, we hired a husky Spanish Republican refugee to be our night watchman. He was full of doglike affection that he expressed by giving us big Spanish hugs that nearly cracked our ribs.

The $10,000 the British Ambassador had given me to spend in evacuating British soldiers was nearly gone. With it we had gotten out about 125 officers and men, including at least one secret agent and a handful of veteran pilots. I sent a message to the British asking for more money to take care of the remaining British soldiers in southern France.

I never got an answer to this request. I was just as glad to no longer be a British agent, for at about this time I learned that the French were collaborating with the Gestapo in tracking down all British espionage activities.

Early in April, Captain Murphy had made a money exchange transaction with Dimitru. The deal yielded him 600,000 francs in cash. The next day Murphy's apartment was robbed, and every franc of the money was taken. Captain Murphy said the only people who knew anything about the money were himself and Dimitru. What part did Dimitru play in the robbery? In May we found out.

Some time in April, Dimitru had given me an opportunity to buy $8,000 in American gold dollars. This was worth about $15,000 in paper currency. The five bags of gold gave us a very handy backlog in case of emergency. At first, we kept the gold in a safe at the Villa Air-Bel, but after we heard of Murphy's robbery, we buried the bags of gold in the pine woods behind the house.

We didn't do this any too soon. One morning early in May, the police arrived at the house before breakfast with a warrant to search the safe for gold and foreign currency. Of course they didn't find any.

But how did they know about the gold?

A week later, Dimitru pointed out that gold dollars were selling at the very high price of 268 francs, and advised me to sell half our gold and take the profit. I said yes right away. We agreed that I would bring the coins to his hotel the next day. But the next day I was so busy that instead of meeting

Dimitru myself, I sent Danny. Since the gold was too heavy to carry all at once, Danny took $2,000 to town and delivered it safely to Dimitru. Then he went back to the house to get the second $2,000.

As he neared Dimitru's hotel with the second load of gold coins in his briefcase, he saw Dimitru standing on the steps, and three suspicious-looking men loitering across the street. Suspecting a trap, he decided to walk right by without speaking to Dimitru or seeming to recognize him. But as he passed the door of the hotel, Dimitru came down the steps and spoke to him.

"I don't like the looks of things," Dimitru said. "Better not bring that stuff in now. Take it back to the house. I'll see you later."

He took Danny's hand in his own empty-glove hand and shook it limply. Then he turned back to the hotel. Immediately the three men crossed the street and showed their badges.

"Let's see what's in that briefcase," one of them said.

Danny opened the briefcase. When they saw what was in it, they arrested him. At the police station they asked him how he got the gold and where he was taking it.

Danny took all the responsibility on himself. He said that Max Ernst, before leaving France, had offered it to me as a gift for the Committee. I had refused it because it was illegal to dispose of gold. Then Max Ernst had offered it to him and knowing how badly the Committee needed the money, he had accepted it without my knowledge, with the intention of changing it into francs and giving the francs to the Committee.

When they had taken his statement, the detectives let him go, but they made him promise to return for more questioning the next day. Danny was convinced that Dimitru had deliberately betrayed him. He insisted that Dimitru had come down the steps of the hotel and spoken to him only to show the detectives whom to arrest.

"He turned me in! He turned me in! I swear, he turned me in!" he said.

The next morning Danny went to the station house to report, as he had promised to do. He didn't come back. I consulted a lawyer and found that Danny had been put in prison. He had been charged with illegal possesion of gold, transporting gold illegally, intention of changing gold illegally, and intention of diverting it to his own use. The total penalties might amount to four or five years in prison.

At the lawyer's suggestion, I went to see the Consul-General at the American Embassy. I explained exactly what had happened, and that it was all my fault. The Embassy intervened with the police, and Danny was freed from prison at last.

Dimitru never gave us back the $2,000 in gold Danny delivered to him. He said the police had searched his room and confiscated it. Our lawyer checked and could find no record of any search. He came back with the conviction that Dimitru was a police agent. A few days later he told us he had learned that Dimitru was also a Gestapo agent.

This made everything quite clear. We knew who had betrayed Danny. We also knew who kept the police informed of all our illegal financial transactions, and who had robbed Murphy.

But what else did Dimitru know — and what had he told the Vichy police and the German Gestapo?

That evening I decided to give Dimitru the scare of his life. Charles, the gangster leader, had frequently boasted that his price for murdering a man was 5,000 francs, with a 20 percent discount if the victim were a policeman.

I got Jean to act as intermediary. He went down to the Dorade and had a talk with Charles about eliminating Dimitru. At first, Charles agreed to do it for the regular price, but as usual there was a delay. Then, later, he said there was a difficulty. Later still, Charles explained that Dimitru had disappeared and, in fact, we found he was no longer in Marseilles. We learned that Dimitru had gone down to the Côte d'Azur. When we told Charles this, he said he would send a man down to deal with Dimitru there.

Weeks passed, and still nothing happened. Finally, pressed for a definite answer, Charles said that Dimitru was very well protected. Murdering him would be exceedingly dangerous. It couldn't be done for less than 100,000 francs.

Of course I knew that it wouldn't be done even for that huge sum. I had not forgotten that Charles and Dimitru were partners. But I thought that by this time we had scared Dimitru enough for him to transfer his attentions elsewhere.

Evidently I was right — he never bothered us again.

33

"Because you have
helped and protected . . ."

After Danny's arrest, everything seemed to go to pieces at once. The British seized one of the Martinique ships as a prize of war, and Vichy immediately canceled all future sailings. They ordered two ships that had already left Marseilles to put in at Casablanca. All the passengers were disembarked and placed in concentration camps. It took months of hard work to get them released and send them on to Spain and Portugal, where they could get passage to America. Meanwhile, Portugal had become so crowded with refugees that virtually no one was able to leave Marseilles for Lisbon.

The police also became bolder in their attitude toward us. One day I picked up the telephone and dialed a number. When I got the number, I could hear a regular "click, click, click" in the receiver. It was unmistakably the sound of a cracked dictaphone cylinder.

The following week, three detectives arrived at

the office with a warrant to look for false passports, false visas, and false identity cards. They made a thorough search, spending more than an hour at it, but they found nothing. We may have been naïve, but we had never been quite stupid enough to keep false documents in the office. Shortly after this episode, the American Consul called me in and warned me that the Gestapo was bringing pressure on the French police to arrest me immediately.

A few days later, at about six o'clock in the evening, a motorcycle dispatch rider arrived at the office with a summons for me from Captain de Rodellec du Porzic to present myself before him the following morning at eleven o'clock sharp. Failure to accept the invitation would result in my immediate arrest.

I arrived at his office promptly at eleven o'clock. Three quarters of an hour later a buzzer sounded, and I was shown into a large office, with a desk at one end of it.

De Rodellec du Porzic motioned to me to sit down in a chair opposite the desk. Then he opened a big dossier, and I could see the blue stationery of my Committee from time to time as he slowly turned over the papers.

Finally, he looked up. "You have caused my good friend the Consul-General of the United States much annoyance," he said.

"I guess the Consul can take care of his own problems," I said.

"My friend the Consul-General tells me that your government and the American committee you represent have both asked you to return to the United States without delay," he continued.

"There's some mistake," I said. "My instructions from my Committee are to stay."

"This affair of your secretary," de Rodellec du Porzic went on, obviously referring to Danny, "will have very serious consequences for you."

"I can't see how," I said. "One of my employees has committed an indiscretion. But he acted entirely on his own responsibility. There is no proof that I was involved in any way."

"In the new France, we do not need proof," de Rodellec du Porzic said. "In the days of the Republic, it used to be believed that it was better to let a hundred criminals escape than to arrest one innocent man. We have done away with all that. We believe it is better to arrest a hundred innocent men than to let one criminal escape."

"I see," I said, "that we are very far apart in our ideas of the rights of man."

"Yes," de Rodellec du Porzic said. "I know that in the United States you still adhere to the old idea of human rights. But you will come to our view in the end. It is merely a question of time. We have realized that society is more important than the individual. You will come to see that, too."

He paused to close the dossier. "When are you leaving France?" he asked.

I said I had no definite plans.

"Unless you leave France of your own free will," he said, "I shall be obliged to arrest you and place you in forced residence in some small town far from

Marseilles, where you can do no harm."

I had to play for time. "I see," I said. "Can you give me a little while to arrange my affairs and get someone over from America to take my place as head of the Committee before I go? I'm willing to go myself, since you insist. But I want to make sure the Committee will go on after I leave."

"Why are you so much interested in your Committee?" he asked.

"Because it is the only hope of many of the refugees."

"I see," he said. "How much time will you need?"

"Well," I said, "I'll cable New York today. It will take them a little time to find someone to replace me, and some more time for my replacement to get his passport and visas and get here. Can you give me until the fifteenth of August?"

"That will be satisfactory," he said.

I got up to go. Then I turned back and asked a final question. "Tell me frankly," I said. "Why are you so much opposed to me?"

"*Parce que vous avez trop protégé des juifs et des anti-Nazis,*" he said. "Because you have helped and protected Jews and anti-Nazis."

I left his office.

34
Good-bye to All That

A day or so after my talk with de Rodellec du Porzic, the Consul handed me my passport, validated for one month, for westbound travel only. The Portuguese and Spanish transit visas and the French exit visa were already in it.

I decided to go to Vichy and see if I could extend my stay. Once again, the Consul warned me not to go. This time, he said, the police would surely arrest me. But nothing happened in Vichy at all — that was the trouble with it. I saw everybody, or at least everybody who would see me. They were all friendly, but no one could do anything. The American Embassy refused to make an inquiry.

"You ought to have gone home a long time ago," was the comment.

The best advice came, as usual, from the American newspapermen. They advised me to stay away from Marseilles until my successor arrived. Their theory was "out of sight, out of mind."

So from Vichy I went on a little "vacation" on the Côte d'Azur. I stayed a week at Sanary-sur-Mer, and Jean came down from Marseilles from time to time to consult with me about the underground railroad through Spain.

Then, because the period of grace he had given me had expired and I was afraid de Rodellec du Porzic might have me arrested if he knew where I was, I moved slowly along the coast. I stayed a day or two at Toulon and St. Tropez and St. Raphael. Then I reached Cannes.

Danny met me at Cannes, and we went on to Nice by train. From there we walked along the Grand Corniche to the Italian demarcation line, just west of Menton. From Menton we took a bus back to Monaco.

I had a strange feeling in Monaco. As soon as you stepped over the line, you could sense that you were no longer in France. It was a wonderful relief, and, once I got there, I didn't want to go away again. For the first time in more than a year, I felt safe from arrest.

But Danny persuaded me that my feeling about being arrested was foolish. "The French police are only bluffing," he said. "They would never dare arrest you."

Finally, I gave in to his pleading, and my own real desire. We took the train back to Marseilles. My visas had expired by that time. I thought I couldn't be expelled.

When I reached the office, I found a cable from New York on my desk. "SUCCESSOR AP-

POINTED MAKING LAST PREPARATIONS TO SEND HIM," it read.

It was Wednesday, August 27, almost two weeks to the day after my period of grace had expired, and still I hadn't been arrested. Perhaps after all, I thought as I settled down to work, de Rodellec du Porzic was only bluffing.

Two days later, just before lunch, two young detectives came to the office with an order signed by de Rodellec. It said they were to take me to Police Headquarters and hold me at his disposal there. No explanation. I was not to be allowed to communicate with anyone. I tried to telephone the Consulate, but even that was forbidden.

At eleven o'clock the next morning, after spending the night sleeping on a table, I was called into the office of the chief and shown an order signed by de Rodellec du Porzic. It said that Varian Fry, being an undesirable alien, was to be conducted to the Spanish frontier immediately and there *refoulé* — pushed out.

When I told him my transit and exit visas had all expired, he called de Rodellec du Porzic's office. They ordered him to send me down to the border anyway, saying the visas would be renewed there. I told him it was impossible to renew visas at the border, but he only shrugged.

"Orders are orders," he said.

Then he presented me to the man who was to accompany me to the frontier. "This is Inspector Garandel," he said. "He is going to take you to the border."

"How do you do," Garandel said, taking my hand. He seemed embarrassed. "It is my duty to show you that we French are not barbarians."

"I never for a moment thought you were," I said.

He smiled. "But the way you have been treated . . . ?" he said.

"Oh, that," I said. "That is just *some* Frenchmen. One might almost say *one* Frenchman. . . ."

He beamed. "Yes," he said. "I'm glad you realize."

At half past three, the same two detectives who had arrested me came to get me. Riding in a large police van, we went first to the office. I emptied the contents of my desk into a paper box and said goodbye to the members of the staff who were still there. Danny had gone to Vichy to try and stop the proceedings, and most of the others, profiting from the lull in work that always followed a raid or an arrest, had gone home for the day. But little Anna Gruss was there and helped me get my things together.

Then we drove out to the Villa Air-Bel. I was given one hour to pack everything I had accumulated in more than a year: clothing, paintings, maps, books, and documents. There was no time for long farewells.

Garandel came to Police Headquarters at six and took me to the railroad station in a police car. When we got to the station, I crossed to the top of the monumental staircase that led down to the Boulevard d'Athènes and the Hotel Splendide. I thought of the first time I had seen it on my arrival in Marseilles. I had come for a month, and now it was almost thirteen months later. So much had happened.

We had a hurried dinner at the station restaurant and then took the train to Narbonne. We arrived there at one o'clock in the morning. Danny arrived from Vichy at eight the next morning. He reported that there was nothing to be done at Vichy. My expulsion had been ordered by the Ministry of the Interior, with the approval of the American Embassy, and neither the Embassy nor the Interior had any intention of reversing it.

At the border, as I had predicted, we were unable to get my visas renewed.

"What's the matter with them up there at Marseilles?" the commissioner said. "They don't seem to know their heads from their tails! You can't get visas here. There aren't any Consulates."

Garandel called Marseilles for instructions. They told him to take me back to Perpignan and hand me over to the local police to be locked up until the visas had been renewed.

"Don't you worry," Garandel said, looking me straight in the eye. "You'll stay in a hotel."

It took five days to get my new transit and exit visas.

The time passed quickly — too quickly. Garandel left me free during the daylight hours, but at night he always stuck close to me until it was time to go to bed.

One evening at dinner, I asked him why he felt he could safely leave me alone with my friends in the daytime but guarded me like a hawk at night.

"After all," I said, "I could just as easily escape during the daytime as at night."

"That is not the question," he said. "But the town is full of Boches. You can never tell what they might do to you on one of these dark streets if you should go out alone at night."

During my free days, there was time to talk over the problems created by my sudden departure. We decided to make Jean the executive director of the Committee, pending the arrival of my successor from New York, for he was the only male member of the staff who had never had any trouble with the police. Danny was to continue running the office, but from behind the scenes.

On Saturday my new visas were ready.

It was gray and rainy as we took the train back to the border. We had our second farewell lunch in the station restaurant. Then, in the station waiting room, surrounded by travel posters and trunks in transit, we took leave of one another. Everybody seemed very much moved, and everybody kissed me good-bye. But it was Danny who seemed the most deeply affected.

He put his arms around me and hugged me. "You can't leave us, my good friend," he whispered. "You've become almost more French than American."

Just then the conductor blew his whistle. *"En voiture!"* the guard cried. "All aboard."

Moments later, we entered the international tunnel.

* * *

It was also raining in Spain, and the trees and fields were wet and sad. During the trip, I looked out of the windows and innumerable images crowded my mind and filled me with a melancholy nostalgia. I thought of the office first, of course, and of my colleagues there. Then of the Villa Air-Bel and of the good company that used to fill it. Of the days on the *Sinaïa*, and the songs we sang, and the tricks we played to get more wine, and the deep anger I felt at being held against my will. I thought of the letters and reports and cables, of messages sent in toothpaste tubes, of passports and visas, real and false, of the concentration camps and the people in them, of the faces of the thousand refugees I had sent out of France, and the faces of a thousand more I had had to leave behind.

It made me very sad. It was partly the land — France. One grows attached to a place very easily, especially when the place is a country as beautiful as France.

But the sadness was much more because of leaving my friends, French and refugee, and the spirit of intimate companionship and devotion to a common cause we had all shared.

35
End of an Assignment

Soon after I got back to New York, Japan attacked Pearl Harbor and the United States entered the war. For a few months the Centre Américain de Secours in Marseilles continued to function and managed to send out nearly three hundred more refugees before it was raided and closed by the police on June 2, 1942.

Almost immediately after the closing of the office there began one of the most grisly manhunts in all history. First in the occupied zone and then in the unoccupied, men, women, and children of Jewish ancestry were rounded up by the police, packed into cattle cars, and sent off to Poland to be exterminated. Bill Freier, the Austrian cartoonist, was among them. By a miracle, he was one of the few to survive.

I would like to be able to end this book by telling you what happened to all of the characters in it. But I can't do that; there were far too many people and I don't know myself what became of most of them.

Some of them, of course, are now a part of the scientific and cultural history of our time. Among the refugees who went on to even more brilliant achievements in their fields were such distinguished figures as Wanda Landowska, the harpsichordist; the painters Marc Chagall, Max Ernst, André Masson, and Wilfredo Lam; the sculptor Jacques Lipchitz; Franz Werfel, author of *The Song of Bernadette*; Fritz Kahn, the medical authority who wrote *Man in Structure and Function*; Alfredo Mendizabel, Spain's leading Catholic philosopher; Jacques Hadamard, the "Einstein of France"; Otto Meyerhoff, Nobel Prize-winning biochemist; Hannah Arendt, the political scientist; and novelist Hans Habe.

Of the refugees who remained in France, many were arrested by the Gestapo and taken to Germany, presumably to be murdered. Many others joined the Resistance, working heroically to undermine the Nazi conquerors and harass the Vichy collaborators.

In 1944, Danny Bénédite, by then a leader of a *maquis* group, was arrested by the Gestapo. After months of imprisonment, he was sentenced to go before a firing squad when the American troops landed in southern France and his life was saved. Jean Gemahling was arrested three times for his underground activities against the Nazis and managed to get away each time. After the war, both

Danny and Jean were made Knights of the Legion of Honor.

Mrs. Anna Gruss, my gnomelike secretary, turned out to be a heroine. Throughout the German occupation she, too, worked in the underground, helping to get money to the refugees and guiding them to the border.

Almost all of those who worked in the Marseilles office went on to further service in the Allied cause. Some, like Beamish, joined the United States Army. Others, like Lena, Franzi, André Breton, and myself, worked on special assignments for the government during the war years. The Office of Strategic Services was particularly interested in our knowledge: The exits to the west set up by our organization became entrances into occupied France and Europe for the O.S.S.

It was a risky assignment, rescuing people. But it had to be done. As Beamish — Professor Albert Hirschman of the Institute for Advanced Study in Princeton — once put it:

"What we tried to do for the refugees in France was like what soldiers have to do in the battle-field — bring the wounded back, no matter the cost. Some may die. Some will be crippled for life. Some will recover and be the better soldiers for having had the experience of battle. But one must bring them all back. At least one must try."